FEMINISM IS FOR EVERYBODY

FEMINISM IS FOR EVERYBODY
Passionate Politics

bell hooks

South End Press
Cambridge, MA

Cover design by Ellen P. Shapiro
Cover illustration by Laura DeSantis, © Artville

Library of Congress Cataloging-in-Publication Data

Hooks, Bell.
Feminism is for everybody : passionate politics / Bell Hooks.
   p. cm.
Includes bibliographical references and index.
ISBN 0-89608-629-1 — ISBN 0-89608-628-3 (pbk.)
1. Feminist theory. 2. Feminism — Philosophy. 3. Feminism — Political aspects. 4. Sex discrimination against women. I. Title.

HQ1190 .H67 2000
305.42'01 — dc21

                                                                00-036589
South End Press, 7 Brookline Street, #1, Cambridge, MA 02139
      06 05 04 03   6 7 8 9

Printed in Canada

CONTENTS

INTRODUCTION
Come Closer to Feminism

Everywhere I go I proudly tell folks who want to know who I am and what I do that I am a writer, a feminist theorist, a cultural critic. I tell them I write about movies and popular culture, analyzing the message in the medium. Most people find this exciting and want to know more. Everyone goes to movies, watches television, glances through magazines, and everyone has thoughts about the messages they receive, about the images they look at. It is easy for the diverse public I encounter to understand what I do as a cultural critic, to understand my passion for writing (lots of folks want to write, and do). But feminist theory — that's the place where the questions stop. Instead I tend to hear all about the evil of feminism and the bad feminists: how "they" hate men; how "they" want to go against nature — and god; how "they" are all lesbians; how "they" are taking all the jobs and making the world hard for white men, who do not stand a chance.

When I ask these same folks about the feminist books or magazines they read, when I ask them about the feminist talks they have heard, about the feminist activists they know, they respond by letting me know that everything they know about feminism has come into their lives thirdhand, that they really have not come close enough to feminist movement to know what really happens, what it's really about. Mostly they think feminism is a bunch of angry women who want to be like men. They do not even think about feminism as being about rights — about women gaining equal rights. When I talk about the feminism I know — up close and personal — they willingly listen, although when our conversations end, they are quick to tell me I am different, not like the "real" feminists who hate men, who are angry. I assure them I am as a real and as radical a feminist as one can be, and if they dare to come closer to feminism they will see it is not how they have imagined it.

Each time I leave one of these encounters, I want to have in my hand a little book so that I can say, read this book, and it will tell you what feminism is, what the movement is about. I want to be holding in my hand a concise, fairly easy to read and understand book; not a long book, not a book thick with hard to understand jargon and academic language, but a straightforward, clear book — easy to read without being simplistic. From the moment feminist thinking, politics, and practice changed my life, I have wanted this book. I have wanted to give it to the folk I love so that they can understand better this cause, this feminist politics I believe in so deeply, that is the foundation of my political life.

I have wanted them to have an answer to the question "what is feminism?" that is rooted neither in fear or fantasy. I have wanted them to have this simple definition to read again and again so they know: "Feminism is a movement to end sexism, sexist exploitation, and oppression." I love this definition, which I first offered more than 10 years ago in my book *Feminist Theory: From Margin to Center*. I love it because it so clearly states that the movement is not about being anti-male. It makes it clear that the problem is sexism. And that clarity helps us remember that all of us, female and male, have been socialized from birth on to accept sexist thought and action. As a consequence, females can be just as sexist as men. And while that does not excuse or justify male domination, it does mean that it would be naive and wrongminded for feminist thinkers to see the movement as simplistically being for women against men. To end patriarchy (another way of naming the institutionalized sexism) we need to be clear that we are all participants in perpetuating sexism until we change our minds and hearts, until we let go of sexist thought and action and replace it with feminist thought and action.

Males as a group have and do benefit the most from patriarchy, from the assumption that they are superior to females and should rule over us. But those benefits have come with a price. In return for all the goodies men receive from patriarchy, they are required to dominate women, to exploit and oppress us, using violence if they must to keep patriarchy intact. Most men find it difficult to be patri-archs. Most men are disturbed by hatred and fear of women, by male violence against women, even the men who perpetuate this vio-lence. But they fear letting go of the benefits. They are not certain what will happen to the world they know most intimately if patriar-chy changes. So they find it easier to passively support male domina-tion even when they know in their minds and hearts that it is wrong. Again and again men tell me they have no idea what it is feminists want. I believe them. I believe in their capacity to change and grow. And I believe that if they knew more about feminism they would no longer fear it, for they would find in feminist movement the hope of their own release from the bondage of patriarchy.

It is for these men, young and old, and for all of us, that I have written this short handbook, the book I have spent more than 20 years longing for. I had to write it because I kept waiting for it to ap-pear, and it did not. And without it there was no way to address the hordes of people in this nation who are daily bombarded with anti-feminist backlash, who are being told to hate and resist a move-ment that they know very little about. There should be so many little feminist primers, easy to read pamphlets and books, telling us all about feminism, that this book would be just another passionate voice speaking out on behalf of feminist politics. There should be billboards; ads in magazines; ads on buses, subways, trains; television commercials spreading the word, letting the world know more about feminism. We are not there yet. But this is what we must do to share feminism, to let the movement into everyone's mind and heart. Feminist change has already touched all our lives in a positive way. And yet we lose sight of the positive when all we hear about feminism is negative.

When I began to resist male domination, to rebel against patriarchal thinking (and to oppose the strongest patriarchal voice in my life — my mother's voice), I was still a teenager, suicidal, depressed, uncertain about how I would find meaning in my life and a place for myself. I needed feminism to give me a foundation of equality and justice to stand on. Mama has come around to feminist thinking. She sees me and all her daughters (we are six) living better lives because of feminist politics. She sees the promise and hope in feminist movement. It is that promise and hope that I want to share with you in this book, with everybody.

Imagine living in a world where there is no domination, where females and males are not alike or even always equal, but where a vision of mutuality is the ethos shaping our interaction. Imagine living in a world where we can all be who we are, a world of peace and possibility. Feminist revolution alone will not create such a world; we need to end racism, class elitism, imperialism. But it will make it possible for us to be fully self-actualized females and males able to create beloved community, to live together, realizing our dreams of freedom and justice, living the truth that we are all "created equal." Come closer. See how feminism can touch and change your life and all our lives. Come closer and know firsthand what feminist movement is all about. Come closer and you will see: feminism is for everybody.

FEMINIST POLITICS
Where We Stand

Simply put, feminism is a movement to end sexism, sexist exploitation, and oppression. This was a definition of feminism I offered in *Feminist Theory: From Margin to Center* more than 10 years ago. It was my hope at the time that it would become a common definition everyone would use. I liked this definition because it did not imply that men were the enemy. By naming sexism as the problem it went directly to the heart of the matter. Practically, it is a definition which implies that all sexist thinking and action is the problem, whether those who perpetuate it are female or male, child or adult. It is also broad enough to include an understanding of systemic institutionalized sexism. As a definition it is open-ended. To understand feminism it implies one has to necessarily understand sexism.

As all advocates of feminist politics know, most people do not understand sexism, or if they do, they think it is not a problem. Masses of people think that feminism is always and only about women seeking to be equal to men. And a huge majority of these folks think feminism is anti-male. Their misunderstanding of feminist politics reflects the reality that most folks learn about feminism from patriarchal mass media. The feminism they hear about the most is portrayed by women who are primarily committed to gender equality — equal pay for equal work, and sometimes women and men sharing household chores and parenting. They see that these women are usually white and materially privileged. They know from mass media that women's liberation focuses on the freedom to have abortions, to be lesbians, to challenge rape and domestic violence. Among these issues, masses of people agree with the idea of gender equity in the workplace — equal pay for equal work.

Since our society continues to be primarily a "Christian" culture, masses of people continue to believe that god has ordained that women be subordinate to men in the domestic household. Even though masses of women have entered the workforce, even though many families are headed by women who are the sole breadwinners, the vision of domestic life which continues to dominate the nation's imagination is one in which the logic of male domination is intact, whether men are present in the home or not. The wrongminded notion of feminist movement which implied it was anti-male carried with it the wrongminded assumption that all female space would necessarily be an environment where patriarchy and sexist thinking would be absent. Many women, even those involved in feminist politics, chose to believe this as well.

There was indeed a great deal of anti-male sentiment among early feminist activists who were responding to male domination with anger. It was that anger at injustice that was the impetus for creating a women's liberation movement. Early on most feminist activists (a majority of whom were white) had their consciousness raised about the nature of male domination when they were working in anti-classist and anti-racist settings with men who were telling the world about the importance of freedom while subordinating the women in their ranks. Whether it was white women working on behalf of socialism, black women working on behalf of civil rights and black liberation, or Native American women working for indigenous rights, it was clear that men wanted to lead, and they wanted women to follow. Participating in these radical freedom struggles awakened the spirit of rebellion and resistance in progressive females and led them towards contemporary women's liberation.

As contemporary feminism progressed, as women realized that males were not the only group in our society who supported sexist thinking and behavior — that females could be sexist as well — anti-male sentiment no longer shaped the movement's consciousness. The focus shifted to an all-out effort to create gender justice. But women could not band together to further feminism without confronting our sexist thinking. Sisterhood could not be powerful as long as women were competitively at war with one another. Utopian visions of sisterhood based solely on the awareness of the reality that all women were in some way victimized by male domination were disrupted by discussions of class and race. Discussions of class differences occurred early on in contemporary feminism, preceding discussions of race. Diana Press published revolutionary insights about class divisions between women as early as the mid-'70s in their collection of essays *Class and Feminism*. These discussions did not trivialize the feminist insistence that "sisterhood is powerful," they simply emphasized that we could only become sisters in struggle by confronting the ways women — through sex, class, and race — dominated and exploited other women, and created a political platform that would address these differences.

Even though individual black women were active in contemporary feminist movement from its inception, they were not the individuals who became the "stars" of the movement, who attracted the attention of mass media. Often individual black women active in feminist movement were revolutionary feminists (like many white lesbians). They were already at odds with reformist feminists who resolutely wanted to project a vision of the movement as being solely about women gaining equality with men in the existing system. Even before race became a talked about issue in feminist circles it was clear to black women (and to their revolutionary allies in struggle) that they were never going to have equality within the existing white supremacist capitalist patriarchy.

From its earliest inception feminist movement was polarized. Reformist thinkers chose to emphasize gender equality. Revolutionary thinkers did not want simply to alter the existing system so that women would have more rights. We wanted to transform that system, to bring an end to patriarchy and sexism. Since patriarchal mass media was not interested in the more revolutionary vision, it never received attention in mainstream press. The vision of "women's liberation" which captured and still holds the public imagination was the one representing women as wanting what men had. And this was the vision that was easier to realize. Changes in our nation's economy, economic depression, the loss of jobs, etc., made the climate ripe for our nation's citizens to accept the notion of gender equality in the workforce.

Given the reality of racism, it made sense that white men were more willing to consider women's rights when the granting of those rights could serve the interests of maintaining white supremacy. We can never forget that white women began to assert their need for freedom after civil rights, just at the point when racial discrimination was ending and black people, especially black males, might have attained equality in the workforce with white men. Reformist feminist thinking focusing primarily on equality with men in the workforce overshadowed the original radical foundations of contemporary feminism which called for reform as well as overall restructuring of society so that our nation would be fundamentally anti-sexist.

Most women, especially privileged white women, ceased even to consider revolutionary feminist visions, once they began to gain economic power within the existing social structure. Ironically, revolutionary feminist thinking was most accepted and embraced in academic circles. In those circles the production of revolutionary feminist theory progressed, but more often than not that theory was not made available to the public. It became and remains a privileged discourse available to those among us who are highly literate, well-educated, and usually materially privileged. Works like *Feminist Theory: From Margin to Center* that offer a liberatory vision of feminist transformation never receive mainstream attention. Masses of people have not heard of this book. They have not rejected its message; they do not know what the message is.

While it was in the interest of mainstream white supremacist capitalist patriarchy to suppress visionary feminist thinking which was not anti-male or concerned with getting women the right to be like men, reformist feminists were also eager to silence these forces. Reformist feminism became their route to class mobility. They could break free of male domination in the workforce and be more self-determining in their lifestyles. While sexism did not end, they could maximize their freedom within the existing system. And they could count on there being a lower class of exploited subordinated women to do the dirty work they were refusing to do. By accepting and indeed colluding with the subordination of working-class and poor women, they not only ally themselves with the existing patriarchy and its concomitant sexism, they give themselves the right to lead a double life, one where they are the equals of men in the workforce and at home when they want to be. If they choose lesbianism they have the privilege of being equals with men in the workforce while using class power to create domestic lifestyles where they can choose to have little or no contact with men.

Lifestyle feminism ushered in the notion that there could be as many versions of feminism as there were women. Suddenly the politics was being slowly removed from feminism. And the assumption prevailed that no matter what a woman's politics, be she conservative or liberal, she too could fit feminism into her existing lifestyle. Obviously this way of thinking has made feminism more acceptable because its underlying assumption is that women can be feminists without fundamentally challenging and changing themselves or the culture. For example, let's take the issue of abortion. If feminism is a movement to end sexist oppression, and depriving females of reproductive rights is a form of sexist oppression, then one cannot be anti-choice and be feminist. A woman can insist she would never choose to have an abortion while affirming her support of the right of women to choose and still be an advocate of feminist politics. She cannot be anti-abortion and an advocate of feminism. Concurrently there can be no such thing as "power feminism" if the vision of power evoked is power gained through the exploitation and oppression of others.

Feminist politics is losing momentum because feminist movement has lost clear definitions. We have those definitions. Let's reclaim them. Let's share them. Let's start over. Let's have T-shirts and bumper stickers and postcards and hip-hop music, television and radio commercials, ads everywhere and billboards, and all manner of printed material that tells the world about feminism. We can share the simple yet powerful message that feminism is a movement to end sexist oppression. Let's start there. Let the movement begin again.

2

CONSCIOUSNESS-RAISING
A Constant Change of Heart

Feminists are made, not born. One does not become an advocate of feminist politics simply by having the privilege of having been born female. Like all political positions one becomes a believer in feminist politics through choice and action. When women first organized in groups to talk together about the issue of sexism and male domination, they were clear that females were as socialized to believe sexist thinking and values as males, the difference being simply that males benefited from sexism more than females and were as a consequence less likely to want to surrender patriarchal privilege. Before women could change patriarchy we had to change ourselves; we had to raise our consciousness.

Revolutionary feminist consciousness-raising emphasized the importance of learning about patriarchy as a system of domination, how it became institutionalized and how it is perpetuated and maintained. Understanding the way male domination and sexism was expressed in everyday life created awareness in women of the ways we were victimized, exploited, and, in worse case scenarios, oppressed. Early on in contemporary feminist movement, consciousness-raising groups often became settings where women simply unleashed pent-up hostility and rage about being victimized, with little or no focus on strategies of intervention and transformation. On a basic level many hurt and exploited women used the consciousness-raising group therapeutically. It was the site where they uncovered and openly revealed the depths of their intimate wounds. This confessional aspect served as a healing ritual. Through consciousness-raising women gained the strength to challenge patriarchal forces at work and at home.

Importantly though, the foundation of this work began with women examining sexist thinking and creating strategies where we would change our attitudes and belief via a conversion to feminist thinking and a commitment to feminist politics. Fundamentally, the consciousness-raising (CR) group was a site for conversion. To build a mass-based feminist movement women needed to organize. The consciousness-raising session, which usually took place in someone's home (rather than public space that had to be rented or donated), was the meeting place. It was the place where seasoned feminist thinkers and activists could recruit new converts.

Importantly, communication and dialogue was a central agenda at the consciousness-raising sessions. In many groups a policy was in place which honored everyone's voice. Women took turns speaking to make sure everyone would be heard. This attempt to create a non-hierarchal model for discussion positively gave every woman a chance to speak but often did not create a context for engaged dialogue. However, in most instances discussion and debate occurred, usually after everyone had spoken at least once. Argumentative discussion was common in CR groups as it was the way we sought to clarify our collective understanding of the nature of male domination. Only through discussion and disagreement could we begin to find a realistic standpoint on gender exploitation and oppression.

As feminist thinking, which emerged first in the context of small groups where individuals often knew each other (they may have worked together and/or were friends), began to be theorized in printed matter so as to reach a wider audience, groups dismantled. The creation of women's studies as an academic discipline provided another setting where women could be informed about feminist thinking and feminist theory. Many of the women who spearheaded the introduction of women's studies classes into colleges and universities had been radical activists in civil rights struggles, gay rights, and early feminist movement. Many of them did not have doctorates, which meant that they entered academic institutions receiving lower pay and working longer hours than their colleagues in other disciplines. By the time younger graduate students joined the effort to legitimize feminist scholarship in the academy we knew that it was important to gain higher degrees. Most of us saw our commitment to women's studies as political action; we were prepared to sacrifice in order to create an academic base for feminist movement.

By the late '70s women's studies was on its way to becoming an accepted academic discipline. This triumph overshadowed the fact that many of the women who had paved the way for the institutionalization of women's studies were fired because they had master's degrees and not doctorates. While some of us returned to graduate school to get PhDs, some of the best and brightest among us did not because they were utterly disillusioned with the university and burnt out from overwork as well as disappointed and enraged that the radical politics undergirding women's studies was being replaced by liberal reformism. Before too long the women's studies classroom had replaced the free-for-all consciousness-raising group. Whereas women from various backgrounds, those who worked solely as housewives or in service jobs, and big-time professional women, could be found in diverse consciousness-raising groups, the academy was and remains a site of class privilege. Privileged white middle-class women who were a numeric majority though not necessarily the radical leaders of contemporary feminist movement often gained prominence because they were the group mass media focused on as representatives of the struggle. Women with revolutionary feminist consciousness, many of them lesbian and from working-class backgrounds, often lost visibility as the movement received mainstream attention. Their displacement became complete once women's studies became entrenched in colleges and universities which are conservative corporate structures. Once the women's studies classroom replaced the consciousness-raising group as the primary site for the transmission of feminist thinking and strategies for social change the movement lost its mass-based potential.

Suddenly more and more women began to either call themselves "feminists" or use the rhetoric of gender discrimination to change their economic status. The institutionalization of feminist studies created a body of jobs both in the world of the academy and in the world of publishing. These career-based changes led to forms of career opportunism wherein women who had never been politically committed to mass-based feminist struggle adopted the stance and jargon of feminism when it enhanced their class mobility. The dismantling of consciousness-raising groups all but erased the notion that one had to learn about feminism and make an informed choice about embracing feminist politics to become a feminist advocate.

Without the consciousness-raising group as a site where women confronted their own sexism towards other women, the direction of feminist movement could shift to a focus on equality in the workforce and confronting male domination. With heightened focus on the construction of woman as a "victim" of gender equality deserving of reparations (whether through changes in discriminatory laws or affirmative action policies) the idea that women needed to first confront their internalized sexism as part of becoming feminist lost currency. Females of all ages acted as though concern for or rage at male domination or gender equality was all that was needed to make one a "feminist." Without confronting internalized sexism women who picked up the feminist banner often betrayed the cause in their interactions with other women.

By the early '80s the evocation of a politicized sisterhood, so crucial at the onset of the feminist movement, lost meaning as the terrain of radical feminist politics was overshadowed by a lifestyle-based feminism which suggested any woman could be a feminist no matter what her political beliefs. Needless to say such thinking has undermined feminist theory and practice, feminist politics. When feminist movement renews itself, reinforcing again and again the strategies that will enable a mass movement to end sexism and sexist exploitation and oppression for everyone, consciousness-raising will once again attain its original importance. Effectively imitating the model of AA meetings, feminist consciousness-raising groups will take place in communities, offering the message of feminist thinking to everyone irrespective of class, race, or gender. While specific groups based on shared identities might emerge, at the end of every month individuals would be in mixed groups.

Feminist consciousness-raising for males is as essential to revo-lutionary movement as female groups. Had there been an emphasis on groups for males that taught boys and men about what sexism is and how it can be transformed, it would have been impossible for mass media to portray the movement as anti-male. It would also have preempted the formation of an anti-feminist men's movement. Often men's groups were formed in the wake of contemporary fem-inism that in no way addressed the issues of sexism and male domi-nation. Like the lifestyle-based feminism aimed at women these groups often became therapeutic settings for men to confront their wounds without a critique of patriarchy or a platform of resistance to male domination. Future feminist movement will not make this mistake. Males of all ages need settings where their resistance to sexism is affirmed and valued. Without males as allies in struggle feminist movement will not progress. As it is we have to do so much work to correct the assumption deeply embedded in the cultural psyche that feminism is anti-male. Feminism is anti-sexism. A male who has divested of male privilege, who has embraced feminist politics, is a worthy comrade in struggle, in no way a threat to feminism, whereas a female who remains wedded to sexist thinking and behavior infiltrating feminist movement is a dangerous threat. Significantly, the most powerful intervention made by consciousness-raising groups was the demand that all females confront their internalized sexism, their allegiance to patriarchal thinking and action, and their commitment to feminist conversion. That intervention is still needed. It remains the necessary step for anyone choosing feminist politics. The enemy within must be transformed before we can confront the enemy outside. The threat, the enemy, is sexist thought and behavior. As long as females take up the banner of feminist politics without addressing and transforming their own sexism, ultimately the movement will be undermined.

3

SISTERHOOD IS STILL POWERFUL

When the slogan "Sisterhood is powerful" was first used, it was awesome. I began my full-fledged participation in feminist movement my sophomore year in college. Attending an all women's college for a year before I transferred to Stanford University, I knew from firsthand experience the difference in female self-esteem and self-assertion in same-sex classrooms versus those where males were present. At Stanford males ruled the day in every classroom. Females spoke less, took less initiative, and often when they spoke you could hardly hear what they were saying. Their voices lacked strength and confidence. And to make matters worse we were told time and time again by male professors that we were not as intelligent as the males, that we could not be "great" thinkers, writers, and so on. These attitudes shocked me since I had come from an all-female environment where our intellectual worth and value was constantly affirmed by the standard of academic excellence our mostly female professors set for us and themselves.

Indeed, I was indebted to my favorite white female English professor who thought I was not getting the academic guidance I needed at our women's college because they did not have an intensified writing program. She encouraged me to attend Stanford. She believed that I would someday be an important thinker and writer.

At Stanford my ability was constantly questioned. I began to doubt myself. Then feminist movement rocked the campus. Female students and professors demanded an end to discrimination based on gender inside and outside the classroom. Wow, it was an intense and awesome time. There I took my first women's studies class with the writer Tillie Olsen, who compelled her students to think first and foremost about the fate of women from working-class backgrounds. There the scholar and one-day biographer of Anne Sexton, Diane Middlebrook, passed out one of my poems in our class on contemporary poetry with no name on it and asked us to identify whether the writer was male or female, an experiment that made us think critically about judging the value of writing on the basis of gender biases. There I began to write my first book at the age of 19, *Ain't I a Woman: Black Women and Feminism.* None of these incredible transformations would have happened without feminist movement creating a foundation for solidarity between women.

That foundation rested on our critique of what we then called "the enemy within," referring to our internalized sexism. We all knew firsthand that we had been socialized as females by patriarchal thinking to see ourselves as inferior to men, to see ourselves as always and only in competition with one another for patriarchal approval, to look upon each other with jealousy, fear, and hatred. Sexist thinking made us judge each other without compassion and punish one another harshly. Feminist thinking helped us unlearn female self-hatred. It enabled us to break free of the hold patriarchal thinking had on our consciousness.

Male bonding was an accepted and affirmed aspect of patriarchal culture. It was simply assumed that men in groups would stick together, support one another, be team players, place the good of the group over individual gain and recognition. Female bonding was not possible within patriarchy; it was an act of treason. Feminist movement created the context for female bonding. We did not bond against men, we bonded to protect our interests as women. When we challenged professors who taught no books by women, it was not because we did not like those professors (we often did); rightly, we wanted an end to gender biases in the classroom and in the curriculum.

The feminist transformations that were taking place in our coed college in the early '70s were taking place as well in the world of home and work. First and foremost feminist movement urged females to no longer see ourselves and our bodies as the property of men. To demand control of our sexuality, effective birth control and reproductive rights, an end to rape and sexual harassment, we needed to stand in solidarity. In order for women to change job discrimination we needed to lobby as a group to change public policy. Challenging and changing female sexist thinking was the first step towards creating the powerful sisterhood that would ultimately rock our nation.

Following in the wake of civil rights revolution feminist movement in the '70s and '80s changed the face of our nation. The feminist activists who made these changes possible cared for the well-being of all females. We understood that political solidarity between females expressed in sisterhood goes beyond positive recognition of the experiences of women and even shared sympathy for common suffering. Feminist sisterhood is rooted in shared commitment to struggle against patriarchal injustice, no matter the form that injustice takes. Political solidarity between women always undermines sexism and sets the stage for the overthrow of patriarchy. Significantly, sisterhood could never have been possible across the boundaries of race and class if individual women had not been willing to divest of their power to dominate and exploit subordinated groups of women. As long as women are using class or race power to dominate other women, feminist sisterhood cannot be fully realized.

As more women begin to opportunistically lay claim to feminism in the '80s without undergoing the feminist consciousness-raising that would have enabled them to divest of their sexism, the patriarchal assumption that the powerful should rule over the weak informed their relations to other women. As women, particularly previously disenfranchised privileged white women, began to acquire class power without divesting of their internalized sexism, divisions between women intensified. When women of color critiqued the racism within the society as a whole and called attention to the ways that racism had shaped and informed feminist theory and practice, many white women simply turned their backs on the vision of sisterhood, closing their minds and their hearts. And that was equally true when it came to the issue of classism among women.

I remember when feminist women, mostly white women with class privilege, debated the issue of whether or not to hire domestic help, trying to come up with a way to not participate in the subordination and dehumanization of less-privileged women. Some of those women successfully created positive bonding between themselves and the women they hired so that there could be mutual advancement in a larger context of inequality. Rather than abandoning the vision of sisterhood, because they could not attain some utopian state, they created a real sisterhood, one that took into account the needs of everyone involved. This was the hard work of feminist solidarity between women. Sadly, as opportunism within feminism intensified, as feminist gains became commonplace and were therefore taken for granted, many women did not want to work hard to create and sustain solidarity.

A large body of women simply abandoned the notion of sisterhood. Individual women who had once critiqued and challenged patriarchy re-aligned themselves with sexist men. Radical women who felt betrayed by the fierce negative competition between women often simply retreated. And at this point feminist movement, which was aimed at positively transforming the lives of all females, became more stratified. The vision of sisterhood that had been the rallying cry of the movement seemed to many women to no longer matter. Political solidarity between women which had been the force putting in place positive change has been and is now consistently undermined and threatened. As a consequence we are as in need of a renewed commitment to political solidarity between women as we were when contemporary feminist movement first began.

When contemporary feminist movement first began we had a vision of sisterhood with no concrete understanding of the actual work we would need to do to make political solidarity a reality. Through experience and hard work, and, yes, by learning from our failures and mistakes, we now have in place a body of theory and shared practice that can teach new converts to feminist politics what must be done to create, sustain, and protect our solidarity. Since masses of young females know little about feminism and many falsely assume that sexism is no longer the problem, feminist education for critical consciousness must be continuous. Older feminist thinkers cannot assume that young females will just acquire knowledge of feminism along the way to adulthood. They require guidance. Overall women in our society are forgetting the value and power of sisterhood. Renewed feminist movement must once again raise the banner high to proclaim anew "Sisterhood is powerful."

Radical groups of women continue our commitment to building sisterhood, to making feminist political solidarity between women an ongoing reality. We continue the work of bonding across race and class. We continue to put in place the anti-sexist thinking and practice which affirms the reality that females can achieve self-actualization and success without dominating one another. And we have the good fortune to know everyday of our lives that sisterhood is concretely possible, that sisterhood is still powerful.

4

FEMINIST EDUCATION FOR CRITICAL CONSCIOUSNESS

Before women's studies classes, before feminist literature, individual women learned about feminism in groups. The women in those groups were the first to begin to create feminist theory which included both an analysis of sexism, strategies for challenging patriarchy, and new models of social interaction. Everything we do in life is rooted in theory. Whether we consciously explore the reasons we have a particular perspective or take a particular action there is also an underlying system shaping thought and practice. In its earliest inception feminist theory had as its primary goal explaining to women and men how sexist thinking worked and how we could challenge and change it.

In those days most of us had been socialized by parents and society to accept sexist thinking. We had not taken time to figure out the roots of our perceptions. Feminist thinking and feminist theory urged us to do that. At first feminist theory was made available by word of mouth or in cheaply put together newsletters and pamphlets. The development of women's publishing (where women wrote, printed, and controlled production on all levels, including marketing) became the site for the dissemination of feminist thinking. While my first book, *Ain't I a Woman: Black Women and Feminism,* written in the '70s and published in 1981, was produced by a small socialist collective, South End Press, at least half of its members were feminist women, and all its members were anti-sexist.

Producing a body of feminist literature coupled with the demand for the recovery of women's history was one of the most powerful and successful interventions of contemporary feminism. In all spheres of literary writing and academic scholarship works by women had historically received little or no attention as a consequence of gender discrimination. Remarkably, when feminist movement exposed biases in curriculum, much of this forgotten and ignored work was rediscovered. The formation of women's studies programs in colleges and universities provided institutional legitimation for academic focus on work by women. Following in the wake of black studies, women's studies became the place where one could learn about gender, about women, from a non-biased perspective.

Contrary to popular stereotypes, professors in women's studies classes did not and do not trash work by men; we intervene on sexist thinking by showing that women's work is often just as good, as interesting, if not more so, as work by men. So-called great literature by men is critiqued only to show the biases present in the assessment of aesthetic value. I have never taken a women's studies course or heard about one where works by men were deemed unimportant or irrelevant. Feminist critiques of all-male canons of scholarship or literary work expose biases based on gender. Importantly, these exposures were central to making a place for the recovery of women's work and a contemporary place for the production of new work by and about women.

Feminist movement gained momentum when it found its way into the academy. In classrooms all over the nation young minds were able to learn about feminist thinking, read the theory, and use it in their academic explorations. When I was a graduate student preparing to write a dissertation, feminist thinking allowed me to choose to write about a black woman writer who was not widely read at the time, Toni Morrison. Very little serious literary scholarship had been done on works by black women writers prior to feminist movement. When Alice Walker acquired fame, she participated in the recovery of the work of writer Zora Neale Hurston, who shortly became the most canonized black woman writer in American literature. Feminist movement created a revolution when it demanded respect for women's academic work, recognition of that work past and present, and an end to gender biases in curriculum and pedagogy.

The institutionalization of women's studies helped spread the word about feminism. It offered a legitimate site for conversion by providing a sustained body of open minds. Students who attended women's studies classes were there to learn. They wanted to know more about feminist thinking. And it was in those classes that many of us awakened politically. I had come to feminist thinking by challenging male domination in our patriarchal household. But simply being the victim of an exploitative or oppressive system and even resisting it does not mean we understand why it's in place or how to change it. My conversion to feminist politics had occurred long before I entered college, but the feminist classroom was the place where I learned feminist thinking and feminist theory. And it was in that space that I received the encouragement to think critically and write about black female experience.

Throughout the '70s the production of feminist thinking and theory was collaborative work in that women were constantly in dialogue about ideas, testing and reshaping our paradigms. Indeed, when black women and other women of color raised the issue of racial biases as a factor shaping feminist thought there was an initial resistance to the notion that much of what privileged class women had identified as true to female experience might be flawed, but over time feminist theory changed. Even though many white women thinkers were able to acknowledge their biases without doing the work of rethinking, this was still an important shift. By the late '80s most feminist scholarship reflected an awareness of race and class differences. Women scholars who were truly committed to feminist movement and feminist solidarity were eager to produce theory that would address the realities of most women.

While academic legitimation was crucial to the advancement of feminist thought, it created a new set of difficulties. Suddenly the feminist thinking that had emerged directly from theory and practice received less attention than theory that was metalinguistic, creating exclusive jargon; it was written solely for an academic audience. It was as if a large body of feminist thinkers banded together to form an elite group writing theory that could be understood only by an "in" crowd.

Women and men outside the academic domain were no longer considered an important audience. Feminist thinking and theory were no longer tied to feminist movement. Academic politics and careerism overshadowed feminist politics. Feminist theory began to be housed in an academic ghetto with little connection to a world outside. Work was and is produced in the academy that is oftentimes visionary, but these insights rarely reach many people. As a consequence the academization of feminist thought in this manner undermines feminist movement via depoliticization. Deradicalized, it is like every other academic discipline with the only difference being the focus on gender.

Literature that helps inform masses of people, that helps individuals understand feminist thinking and feminist politics, needs to be written in a range of styles and formats. We need work that is especially geared towards youth culture. No one produces this work in academic settings. Without abandoning women's studies programs which are already at risk at colleges and universities as conservatives seek to undo the changes created by struggles for gender justice, we need feminist studies that is community-based. Imagine a mass-based feminist movement where folks go door to door passing out literature, taking the time (as do religious groups) to explain to people what feminism is all about.

When contemporary feminist movement was at its peak, sexist biases in books for children were critiqued. Books "for free children" were written. Once we ceased being critically vigilant, the sexism began to reappear. Children's literature is one of the most crucial sites for feminist education for critical consciousness precisely because beliefs and identities are still being formed. And more often than not narrow-minded thinking about gender continues to be the norm on the playground. Public education for children has to be a place where feminist activists continue to do the work of creating an unbiased curriculum.

Future feminist movement must necessarily think of feminist education as significant in the lives of everyone. Despite the economic gains of individual feminist women, many women who have amassed wealth or accepted the contribution of wealthy males, who are our allies in struggle, we have created no schools founded on feminist principles for girls and boys, for women and men. By failing to create a mass-based educational movement to teach everyone about feminism we allow mainstream patriarchal mass media to remain the primary place where folks learn about feminism, and most of what they learn is negative. Teaching feminist thought and theory to everyone means that we have to reach beyond the academic and even the written word. Masses of folks lack the skills to read most feminist books. Books on tape, songs, radio, and television are all ways to share feminist knowledge. And of course we need a feminist television network, which is not the same as a network for women. Galvanizing funds to create a feminist television network would help us spread feminist thinking globally. If we cannot own a network, let's pay for time on an existing network. After years of ownership by males who were not all anti-sexist *Ms.* magazine is now owned by women who are all deeply committed to feminist principles. This is a step in the right direction.

If we do not work to create a mass-based movement which offers feminist education to everyone, females and males, feminist theory and practice will always be undermined by the negative information produced in most mainstream media. The citizens of this nation cannot know the positive contributions feminist movement has made to all our lives if we do not highlight these gains. Constructive feminist contributions to the well-being of our communities and society are often appropriated by the dominant culture which then projects negative representations of feminism. Most people have no understanding of the myriad ways feminism has positively changed all our lives. Sharing feminist thought and practice sustains feminist movement. Feminist knowledge is for everybody.

5

OUR BODIES, OURSELVES
Reproductive Rights

When contemporary feminist movement began the issues that were projected as most relevant were those that were directly linked to the experiences of highly educated white women (most of whom were materially privileged.) Since feminist movement followed in the wake of civil rights and sexual liberation it seemed appropriate at the time that issues around the female body were foregrounded. Contrary to the image the mass media presented to the world, a feminist movement starting with women burning bras at a Miss America pageant and then later images of women seeking abortions, one of the first issues which served as a catalyst for the formation of the movement was sexuality — the issue being the rights of women to choose when and with whom they would be sexual. The sexual exploitation of women's bodies had been a common occurrence in radical movements for social justice whether socialist, civil rights, etc.

When the so-called sexual revolution was at its peak the issue of free love (which usually meant having as much sex as one wanted with whomever one desired) brought females face to face with the issue of unwanted pregnancy. Before there could be any gender equity around the issue of free love women needed access to safe, effective contraceptives and abortions. While individual white women with class privilege often had access to both these safeguards, most women did not. Often individual women with class privilege were too ashamed of unwanted pregnancy to make use of their more direct access to responsible health care. The women of the late '60s and early '70s who clamored for abortions had seen the tragedies of illegal abortions, the misery of forced marriages as a consequence of unwanted pregnancies. Many of us were the unplanned children of talented, creative women whose lives had been changed by unplanned and unwanted pregnancies; we witnessed their bitterness, their rage, their disappointment with their lot in life. And we were clear that there could be no genuine sexual liberation for women and men without better, safer contraceptives — without the right to a safe, legal abortion.

In retrospect, it is evident that highlighting abortion rather than reproductive rights as a whole reflected the class biases of the women who were at the forefront of the movement. While the issue of abortion was and remains relevant to all women, there were other reproductive issues that were just as vital which needed attention and might have served to galvanize masses. These issues ranged from basic sex education, prenatal care, preventive health care that would help females understand how their bodies worked, to forced sterilization, unnecessary cesareans and/or hysterectomies, and the medical complications they left in their wake. Of all these issues individual white women with class privilege identified most intimately with the pain of unwanted pregnancy. And they highlighted the abortion issue. They were not by any means the only group in need of access to safe, legal abortions. As already stated, they were far more likely to have the means to acquire an abortion than poor and working-class women. In those days poor women, black women included, often sought illegal abortions. The right to have an abortion was not a white-women-only issue; it was simply not the only or even the most important reproductive concern for masses of American women.

The development of effective though not totally safe birth control pills (created by male scientists, most of whom were not anti-sexist) truly paved the way for female sexual liberation more so than abortion rights. Women like myself who were in our late teens when the pill was first widely available were spared the fear and shame of unwanted pregnancies. Responsible birth control liberated many women like myself who were pro-choice but not necessarily pro-abortion for ourselves from having to personally confront the issue. While I never had an unwanted pregnancy in the heyday of sexual liberation, many of my peers saw abortion as a better choice than conscious, vigilant use of birth control pills. And they did frequently use abortion as a means of birth control. Using the pill meant a woman was directly confronting her choice to be sexually active. Women who were more conscientious about birth control were often regarded as sexually loose by men. It was easier for some females just to let things happen sexually then take care of the "problem" later with abortions. We now know that both repeated abortions or prolonged use of birth control pills with high levels of estrogen are not risk-free. Yet women were willing to take risks to have sexual freedom — to have the right to choose.

The abortion issue captured the attention of mass media because it really challenged the fundamentalist thinking of Christianity. It directly challenged the notion that a woman's reason for existence was to bear children. It called the nation's attention to the female body as no other issue could have done. It was a direct challenge to the church. Later all the other reproductive issues that feminist thinkers called attention to were often ignored by mass media. The long-range medical problems from cesareans and hysterectomies were not juicy subjects for mass media; they actually called attention to a capitalist patriarchal male-dominated medical system that controlled women's bodies and did with them anything they wanted to do. To focus on gender injustice in these arenas would have been too radical for a mass media which remains deeply conservative and for the most part anti-feminist.

No feminist activists in the late '60s and early '70s imagined that we would have to wage a battle for women's reproductive rights in the '90s. Once feminist movement created the cultural revolution which made the use of relatively risk-free contraceptives acceptable and the right to have a safe, legal abortion possible women simply assumed those rights would no longer be questioned. The demise of an organized, radical feminist mass-based political movement coupled with anti-feminist backlash from an organized right-wing political front which relies on fundamentalist interpretations of religion placed abortion back on the political agenda. The right of females to choose is now called into question.

Sadly the anti-abortion platform has most viciously targeted state-funded, inexpensive, and, when need be, free abortions. As a consequence women of all races who have class privilege continue to have access to safe abortions — continue to have the right to choose — while materially disadvantaged women suffer. Masses of poor and working-class women lose access to abortion when there is no government funding available for reproductive rights health care. Women with class privilege do not feel threatened when abortions can be had only if one has lots of money because they can still have them. But masses of women do not have class power. More women than ever before are entering the ranks of the poor and indigent. Without the right to safe, inexpensive, and free abortions they lose all control over their bodies. If we return to a world where abortions are only accessible to those females with lots of money we risk the return of public policy that will aim to make abortion illegal. It's already happening in many conservative states. Women of all classes must continue to make abortions safe, legal, and affordable.

The right of women to choose whether or not to have an abortion is only one aspect of reproductive freedom. Depending on a woman's age and circumstance of life the aspect of reproductive rights that matters most will change. A sexually active woman in her 20s or 30s who finds birth control pills unsafe may one day face an unwanted pregnancy and the right to have a legal, safe, inexpensive abortion may be the reproductive issue that is most relevant. But when she is menopausal and doctors are urging her to have a hysterectomy that may be the most relevant reproductive rights issue.

As we seek to rekindle the flames of mass-based feminist movement reproductive rights will remain a central feminist agenda. If women do not have the right to choose what happens to our bodies we risk relinquishing rights in all other areas of our lives. In renewed feminist movement the overall issue of reproductive rights will take precedence over any single issue. This does not meant that the push for legal, safe, inexpensive abortions will not remain central, it will simply not be the only issue that is centralized. If sex education, preventive health care, and easy access to contraceptives are offered to every female, fewer of us will have unwanted pregnancies. As a consequence the need for abortions would diminish.

Losing ground on the issue of legal, safe, inexpensive abortion means that women lose ground on all reproductive issues. The anti-choice movement is fundamentally anti-feminist. While it is possible for women to individually choose never to have an abortion, allegiance to feminist politics means that they still are pro-choice, that they support the right of females who need abortions to choose whether or not to have them. Young females who have always had access to effective contraception — who have never witnessed the tragedies caused by illegal abortions — have no firsthand experience of the powerlessness and vulnerability to exploitation that will always be the outcome if females do not have reproductive rights.

Ongoing discussion about the wide range of issues that come under the heading of reproductive rights is needed if females of all ages and our male allies in struggle are to understand why these rights are important. This understanding is the basis of our commitment to keeping reproductive rights a reality for all females. Feminist focus on reproductive rights is needed to protect and sustain our freedom.

6

BEAUTY WITHIN AND WITHOUT

Challenging sexist thinking about the female body was one of the most powerful interventions made by contemporary feminist movement. Before women's liberation all females young and old were socialized by sexist thinking to believe that our value rested solely on appearance and whether or not we were perceived to be good looking, especially by men. Understanding that females could never be liberated if we did not develop healthy self-esteem and self-love feminist thinkers went directly to the heart of the matter — critically examining how we feel and think about our bodies and offering constructive strategies for change. Looking back after years of feeling comfortable choosing whether or not to wear a bra, I can remember what a momentous decision this was 30 years ago. Women stripping their bodies of unhealthy and uncomfortable, restrictive clothing — bras, girdles, corsets, garter belts, etc. — was a ritualistic, radical reclaiming of the health and glory of the female body. Females today who have never known such restrictions can only trust us when we say that this reclaiming was momentous.

On a deeper level this ritual validated women wearing comfortable clothing on all levels in our lives. Just to be able to wear pants to work was awesome to many women, whose jobs had required them to be constantly bending and stooping over. For women who had never been comfortable in dresses and skirts all these changes were exciting. Today they can appear trivial to females who have been able to freely choose what they want to wear from childhood on. Many adult women embracing feminism stopped wearing crippling, uncomfortable high-heeled shoes. These changes led the shoe-making industry to design comfortable low shoes for women. No longer forced by sexist tradition to wear make-up, women looked in the mirror and learned to face ourselves just the way we are.

The clothing and revolution created by feminist interventions let females know that our flesh was worthy of love and adoration in its natural state; nothing had to be added unless a woman chose further adornment. Initially, capitalist investors in the cosmetic and fashion industry feared that feminism would destroy their business. They put their money behind mass-media campaigns which trivialized women's liberation by portraying images which suggested feminists were big, hypermasculine, and just plain old ugly. In reality, women involved in feminist movement came in all shapes and sizes. We were utterly diverse. And how thrilling to be free to appreciate our differences without judgment or competition.

There was a period in the early days of feminism when many activists abdicated all interest in fashion and appearance. These individuals often harshly critiqued any woman who showed an interest in frilly feminine attire or make-up. Most of us were excited to have options. And given choice, we usually decided in the direction of comfort and ease. It has never been a simple matter for women to unite a love of beauty and style with comfort and ease. Women had to demand that the fashion industry (which was totally male-dominated in those days) create diverse styles of clothing. Magazines changed (feminist activists called for more women writers and articles on serious subjects). For the first time in our nation's history women were compelled to acknowledge the strength of our consumer dollars, using that power to create positive change.

Challenging the industry of sexist-defined fashion opened up the space for females to examine for the first time in our lives the pathological, life-threatening aspects of appearance obsession. Compulsive eating and compulsive starvation were highlighted. While they created different "looks," these life-threatening addictions had the same root. Feminist movement compelled the sexist medical establishment to pay attention to these issues. Initially this establishment ignored feminist critique. But when feminists began to create health centers, providing a space for female-centered, positive health care, the medical industry realized that, as with fashion, masses of women would take their consumer dollars and move in the direction of those health care facilities which provided the greater care, ease, and respect for women's bodies. All the positive changes in the medical establishment's attitudes towards the female body, towards female health care, are the direct outcome of feminist struggle. When it comes to the issue of medical care, of taking our bodies seriously, women continue to challenge and confront the medical industry. This is one of the few places where feminist struggle garners mass support from women, whether they are or are not committed to feminist politics. We see the collective power of women when it comes to gynecological matters, to those forms of cancer (especially breast cancer) that threaten females more than males, and more recently in the area of heart disease.

Feminist struggle to end eating disorders has been an ongoing battle because our nation's obsession with judging females of all ages on the basis of how we look was never completely eliminated. It continues to grip our cultural imagination. By the early '80s many women were moving away from feminism. While all females reaped the benefits of feminist interventions, more and more females were embracing anew sexist-defined notions of beauty. Individual women who had been in their early 20s when contemporary feminist movement began were moving into their late 40s and 50s. Even though feminist changes in the way we see female bodies have made aging a more positive experience for women, facing the reality of aging in patriarchal society, particularly the reality of no longer being able biologically to bear children, led many women to adopt anew the old sexist notions of feminine beauty.

Nowadays, more than ever before in our nation's history, a huge number of heterosexual women past 40 were and are still single. Finding themselves in competition with younger women (many of whom are not and will never be feminist) for male attention they often emulate sexist representations of female beauty. Certainly it was in the interest of a white supremacist capitalist patriarchal fashion and cosmetic industry to re-glamorize sexist-defined notions of beauty. Mass media has followed suit. In movies, on television, and in public advertisements images of reed-thin, dyed-blonde women looking as though they would kill for a good meal have become the norm. Back with a vengeance, sexist images of female beauty abound and threaten to undo much of the progress gained by feminist interventions.

Tragically, even though females are more aware than ever before of the widespread problem of life-threatening eating disorders in our nation's history, a large group of females from the very young to the very old are still starving themselves to be thin. The disease of anorexia has become a commonplace theme, a subject in books, movies, etc. But no dire warnings work to deter females who believe their worth, beauty, and intrinsic value will be determined by whether or not they are thin. Today's fashion magazines may carry an article about the dangers of anorexia while bombarding its readers with images of emaciated young bodies representing the height of beauty and desirability. The confusing message is most damaging to those females who have never claimed a feminist politics. Yet there are recent feminist interventions aimed at renewing our efforts to affirm the natural beauty of female bodies.

Girls today are often just as self-hating when it comes to their bodies as their pre-feminist counterparts were. While feminist movement produced many types of pro-female magazines, no feminist-oriented fashion magazine appeared to offer all females alternative visions of beauty. To critique sexist images without offering alternatives is an incomplete intervention. Critique in and of itself does not lead to change. Indeed, much feminist critique of beauty has merely left females confused about what a healthy choice is. As a middle-aged woman gaining more weight than ever before in my life, I want to work at shedding pounds without deploying sexist body self-hatred to do so. Nowadays, in a fashion world, especially on the consumer side, where clothing that looks like it has been designed simply for reed-thin adolescent girl bodies is the norm, all females no matter their age are being socialized either consciously or unconsciously to have anxiety about their body, to see flesh as problematic. While we are fortunate that some stores carry beautiful clothing for women of all sizes and shapes, often this clothing is far more pricey than the cheaper clothing the fashion industry markets towards the general public. Increasingly today's fashion magazines look like the magazines of the past. More and more bylines are by males. Seldom do articles have a feminist perspective or feminist content. And the fashions portrayed tend to reflect sexist sensibility.

These changes have been unacknowledged publicly because so many of the feminist women who have come to mature adulthood exercise their freedom of choice and seek healthy alternative models of beauty. However, if we abandon the struggle to eliminate sexist defined notions of beauty altogether, we risk undermining all the marvelous feminist interventions which allowed us to embrace our bodies and ourselves and love them. Although all females are more aware of the pitfalls and dangers of embracing sexist notions of female beauty, we are not doing enough to eliminate those dangers — to create alternatives.

Young girls and adolescents will not know that feminist thinkers acknowledge both the value of beauty and adornment if we continue to allow patriarchal sensibilities to inform the beauty industry in all spheres. Rigid feminist dismissal of female longings for beauty has undermined feminist politics. While this sensibility is more uncommon, it is often presented by mass media as the way feminists think. Until feminists go back to the beauty industry, go back to fashion, and create an ongoing, sustained revolution, we will not be free. We will not know how to love our bodies as ourselves.

7

FEMINIST CLASS STRUGGLE

Class difference and the way in which it divides women was an issue women in feminist movement talked about long before race. In the mostly white circles of a newly formed women's liberation movement the most glaring separation between women was that of class. White working-class women recognized that class hierarchies were present in the movement. Conflict arose between the reformist vision of women's liberation which basically demanded equal rights for women within the existing class structure, and more radical and/or revolutionary models, which called for fundamental change in the existing structure so that models of mutuality and equality could replace the old paradigms. However, as feminist movement progressed and privileged groups of well-educated white women began to achieve equal access to class power with their male counterparts, feminist class struggle was no longer deemed important.

From the onset of the movement women from privileged classes were able to make their concerns "the" issues that should be focused on in part because they were the group of women who received public attention. They attracted mass media. The issues that were most relevant to working women or masses of women were never highlighted by mainstream mass media. Betty Friedan's *The Feminist Mystique* identified "the problem that has no name" as the dissatisfaction females felt about being confined and subordinated in the home as housewives. While this issue was presented as a crisis for women it really was only a crisis for a small group of well-educated white women. While they were complaining about the dangers of confinement in the home a huge majority of women in the nation were in the workforce. And many of these working women, who put in long hours for low wages while still doing all the work in the domestic household would have seen the right to stay home as "freedom."

It was not gender discrimination or sexist oppression that kept privileged women of all races from working outside the home, it was the fact that the jobs that would have been available to them would have been the same low-paying unskilled labor open to all working women. Elite groups of highly educated females stayed at home rather than do the type of work large numbers of lower-middle-class and working-class women were doing. Occasionally, a few of these women defied convention and worked outside the home performing tasks way below their educational skills and facing resistance from husbands and family. It was this resistance that turned the issue of their working outside the home into an issue of gender discrimination and made opposing patriarchy and seeking equal rights with men of their class the political platform that chose feminism rather than class struggle.

From the outset, reformist white women with class privilege were well aware that the power and freedom they wanted was the freedom they perceived men of their class enjoying. Their resistance to patriarchal male domination in the domestic household provided them with a connection they could use to unite across class with other women who were weary of male domination. But only privileged women had the luxury to imagine working outside the home would actually provide them with an income which would enable them to be economically self-sufficient. Working-class women already knew that the wages they received would not liberate them.

Reformist efforts on the part of privileged groups of women to change the workforce so that women workers would be paid more and face less gender-based discrimination and harassment on the job had positive impact on the lives of all women. And these gains are important. Yet the fact that the privileged gained in class power while masses of women still do not receive wage equity with men is an indication of the way in which class interests superceded feminist efforts to change the workforce so that women would receive equal pay for equal work.

Lesbian feminist thinkers were among the first activists to raise the issue of class in feminist movement expressing their viewpoints in an accessible language. They were a group of women who had not imagined they could depend on husbands to support them. And they were often much more aware than their straight counterparts of the difficulties all women would face in the workforce. In the early '70s anthologies like *Class and Feminism,* edited by Charlotte Bunch and Nancy Myron, published work written by women from diverse class backgrounds who were confronting the issue in feminist circles. Each essay emphasized the fact that class was not simply a question of money. In "The Last Straw," Rita Mae Brown (who was not a famous writer at the time) clearly stated:

> Class is much more than Marx's definition of relationship to the means of production. Class involved your behavior, your basic assumptions, how you are taught to behave, what you expect from yourself and from others, your concept of a future, how you understand problems and solve them, how you think, feel, act.

These women who entered feminist groups made up of diverse classes were among the first to see that the vision of a politically based sisterhood where all females would unite together to fight patriarchy could not emerge until the issue of class was confronted.

Placing class on feminist agendas opened up the space where the intersections of class and race were made apparent. Within the institutionalized race, sex, class social system in our society black females were clearly at the bottom of the economic totem pole. Initially, well-educated white women from working-class backgrounds were more visible than black females of all classes in feminist movement. They were a minority within the movement, but theirs was the voice of experience. They knew better than their privileged- class comrades of any race the costs of resisting race, class, and gender domination. They knew what it was like to struggle to change one's economic situation. Between them and their privileged-class comrades there were ongoing conflicts over appropriate behavior, over the issues that would be presented as fundamental feminist concerns. Within feminist movement women from privileged-class backgrounds who had never before been involved in leftist freedom fighting learned the concrete politics of class struggle, confronting challenges made by less privileged women, and also learning in the process assertiveness skills and constructive ways to cope with conflict. Despite constructive intervention many privileged white women continued to act as though feminism belonged to them, as though they were in charge.

Mainstream patriarchy reinforced the idea that the concerns of women from privileged-class groups were the only ones worthy of receiving attention. Feminist reform aimed to gain social equality for women within the existing structure. Privileged women wanted equality with men of their class. Despite sexism among their class they would not have wanted to have the lot of working class men. Feminist efforts to grant women social equality with men of their class neatly coincided with white supremacist capitalist patriarchal fears that white power would diminish if nonwhite people gained equal access to economic power and privilege. Supporting what in effect became white power reformist feminism enabled the mainstream white supremacist patriarchy to bolster its power while simultaneously undermining the radical politics of feminism.

Only revolutionary feminist thinkers expressed outrage at this cooptation of feminist movement. Our critique and outrage gained a hearing the alternative press. In her collection of essays, *The Coming of Black Genocide,* radical white activist Mary Barfoot boldly stated:

> There are white women, hurt and angry, who believed that the '70s women's movement meant sisterhood, and who feel betrayed by escalator women. By women who went back home to the patriarchy. But the women's movement never left the father Dick's side.... There was no war. And there was no liberation. We got a share of genocide profits and we love it. We are Sisters of Patriarchy, and true supporters of national and class oppression, Patriarchy in its highest form is Euro-imperialism on a world scale. If we're Dick's sister and want what he has gotten, then in the end we support that system that he got it all from.

Indeed, many more feminist women found and find it easier to consider divesting of white supremacist thinking than of their class elitism.

As privileged women gained greater access to economic power with men of their class feminist discussions of class were no longer commonplace. Instead, all women were encouraged to see the economic gains of affluent females as a positive sign for all women. In actuality, these gains rarely changed the lot of poor and working-class women. And since privileged men did not become equal caretakers in the domestic household, the freedom of privileged-class women of all races has required the sustained subordination of working-class and poor women. In the '90s collusion with the existing social structure was the price of "women's liberation." At the end of the day class power proved to be more important than feminism. And this collusion helped destabilize feminist movement.

When women acquired greater class status and power without conducting themselves differently from males feminist politics were undermined. Lots of women felt betrayed. Middle- and lower-middle-class women who were suddenly compelled by the ethos of feminism to enter the workforce did not feel liberated once they faced the hard truth that working outside the home did not mean work in the home would be equally shared with male partners. No-fault divorce proved to be more economically beneficial to men than women. As many black women/women of color saw white women from privileged classes benefiting economically more than other groups from reformist feminist gains, from gender being tacked on to racial affirmative action, it simply reaffirmed their fear that feminism was really about increasing white power. The most profound betrayal of feminist issues has been the lack of mass-based feminist protest challenging the government's assault on single mothers and the dismantling of the welfare system. Privileged women, many of whom call themselves feminists, have simply turned away from the "feminization of poverty."

The voices of "power feminism" tend to be highlighted in mass media far more than the voices of individual feminist women who have gained class power without betraying our solidarity towards those groups without class privilege. Being true to feminist politics, our goals were and are to become economically self-sufficient and to find ways to assist other women in their efforts to better themselves economically. Our experiences counter the assumption that women can only gain economically by acting in collusion with the existing capitalist patriarchy. All over this nation individual feminists with class power who support a revolutionary vision of social change share resources and use our power to aid reforms that will improve the lives of women irrespective of class.

The only genuine hope of feminist liberation lies with a vision of social change which challenges class elitism. Western women have gained class power and greater gender inequality because a global white supremacist patriarchy enslaves and/or subordinates masses of third-world women. In this country the combined forces of a booming prison industry and workfare-oriented welfare in conjunction with conservative immigration policy create and condone the conditions for indentured slavery. Ending welfare will create a new underclass of women and children to be abused and exploited by the existing structures of domination.

Given the changing realities of class in our nation, widening gaps between the rich and poor, and the continued feminization of poverty, we desperately need a mass-based radical feminist movement that can build on the strength of the past, including the positive gains generated by reforms, while offering meaningful interrogation of existing feminist theory that was simply wrongminded while offering us new strategies. Significantly a visionary movement would ground its work in the concrete conditions of working-class and poor women. That means creating a movement that begins education for critical consciousness where women, feminist women with class power, need to put in place low-income housing women can own. The creation of housing co-ops with feminist principles would show the ways feminist struggle is relevant to all women's lives.

When women with class power opportunistically use a feminist platform while undermining feminist politics that help keep in place a patriarchal system that will ultimately re-subordinate them, they do not just betray feminism; they betray themselves. Returning to a discussion of class, feminist women and men will restore the conditions needed for solidarity. We will then be better able to envision a world where resources are shared and opportunities for personal growth abound for everyone irrespective of their class.

8

GLOBAL FEMINISM

Individual female freedom fighters all over the world have single-handedly struggled against patriarchy and male domination. Since the first people on the planet earth were nonwhite it is unlikely that white women were the first females to rebel against male domination. In white supremacist capitalist patriarchal Western culture neocolonial thinking sets the tone for many cultural practices. That thinking always focuses on who has conquered a territory, who has ownership, who has the right to rule. Contemporary feminist politics did not come into being as a radical response to neocolonialism.

Privileged-class white women swiftly declared their "ownership" of the movement, placing working-class white women, poor white women, and all women of color in the position of followers. It did not matter how many working-class white women or individual black women spearheaded the women's movement in radical directions. At the end of the day white women with class power declared that they owned the movement, that they were the leaders and the rest of merely followers. Parasitic class relations have overshadowed issues of race, nation, and gender in contemporary neocolonialism. And feminism did not remain aloof from that dynamic.

Initially when feminist leaders in the United States proclaimed the need for gender equality here they did not seek to find out if corresponding movements were taking place among women around the world. Instead they declared themselves liberated and therefore in the position to liberate their less fortunate sisters, especially those in the "third world." This neocolonial paternalism had already been enacted to keep women of color in the background so that only conservative/liberal white women would be the authentic representatives of feminism. Radical white women tend not to be "represented," and, if represented at all, they are depicted as a fringe freak element. No wonder then that the "power feminism" of the '90s offers wealthy white heterosexual women as the examples of feminist success.

In truth their hegemonic takeover of feminist rhetoric about equality has helped mask their allegiance to the ruling classes within white supremacist capitalist patriarchy. Radical feminists were dismayed to witness so many women (of all races) appropriating feminist jargon while sustaining their commitment to Western imperialism and transnational capitalism. While feminists in the United States were right to call attention to the need for global equality for women, problems arose as those individual feminists with class power projected imperialist fantasies onto women globally, the major fantasy being that women in the United States have more rights than any group of women globally, are "free" if they want to be, and therefore have the right to lead feminist movement and set feminist agendas for all the other women in the world, particularly women in third world countries. Such thinking merely mirrors the imperialist racism and sexism of ruling groups of Western men.

Most women in the United States do not even know or use the terms colonialism and neocolonialism. Most American women, particularly white women, have not decolonized their thinking either in relation to the racism, sexism, and class elitism they hold towards less powerful groups of women in this society or the masses of women globally. When unenlightened individual feminist thinkers addressed global issues of gender exploitation and oppression they did and do so from a perspective of neocolonialism. Significantly, radical white women writing in *Night-Vision: Illuminating War and Class on the Neo-Colonial Terrain* emphasize the reality that " to not understand neocolonialism is to not fully live in the present." Since unenlightened white feminists were unwilling to acknowledge the spheres of American life where they acted and act in collusion with imperialist white supremacist capitalist patriarchy, sustained protest and resistance on the part of black women/women of color and our radical white sisters was needed to break the wall of denial.

Yet even when large numbers of feminist activists adopted a perspective which included race, gender, class, and nationality, the white "power feminists" continued to project an image of feminism that linked and links women's equality with imperialism. Global women's issues like forced female circumcision, sex clubs in Thailand, the veiling of women in Africa, India, the Middle East, and Europe, the killing of female children in China, remain important concerns. However feminist women in the West are still struggling to decolonize feminist thinking and practice so that these issues can be addressed in a manner that does not reinscribe Western imperialism. Consider the way many Western women, white and black, have confronted the issue of female circumcision in Africa and the Middle East. Usually these countries are depicted as "barbaric and uncivilized," the sexism there portrayed as more brutal and dangerous to women than the sexism here in the United States.

A decolonized feminist perspective would first and foremost examine how sexist practices in relation to women's bodies globally are linked. For example: linking circumcision with life-threatening eating disorders (which are the direct consequence of a culture imposing thinness as a beauty ideal) or any life-threatening cosmetic surgery would emphasize that the sexism, the misogyny, underlying these practices globally mirror the sexism here in this country. When issues are addressed in this manner Western imperialism is not reinscribed and feminism cannot be appropriated by transnational capitalism as yet another luxury product from the West women in other cultures must fight to have the right to consume.

Until radical women in the United States challenge those groups of women posing as feminists in the interest of class opportunism, the tone of global feminism in the West will continue to be set by those with the greatest class power who hold old biases. Radical feminist work around the world daily strengthens political solidarity between women beyond the boundaries of race/ethnicity and nationality. Mainstream mass media rarely calls attention to these positive interventions. In *Hatreds: Racialized and Sexualized Conflicts in the 21st Century,* Zillah Eisenstein shares the insight:

> Feminism(s) as transnational — imagined as the rejection of false race/gender borders and falsely constructed "other" — is a major challenge to masculinist nationalism, the distortions of statist communism and "free"-market globalism. It is a feminism that recognizes individual diversity, and freedom, and equality, defined through and beyond north/west and south/east dialogues.

No one who has studied the growth of global feminism can deny the important work women are doing to ensure our freedom. No one can deny that Western women, particularly women in the United States, have contributed much that is needed to this struggle and need to contribute more. The goal of global feminism is to reach out and join global struggles to end sexism, sexist exploitation, and oppression.

9

WOMEN AT WORK

More than half of all women in the United States are in the workforce. When contemporary feminist movement first began the workforce was already more than one-third female. Coming from a working-class, African-American background where most women I knew were in the workforce, I was among the harshest critics of the vision of feminism put forth by reformist thinkers when the movement began, which suggested that work would liberate women from male domination. More than 10 years ago I wrote in *Feminist Theory: From Margin to Center*. "The emphasis on work as the key to women's liberation led many white feminist activists to suggest women who worked were 'already liberated.' They were in effect saying to the majority of working women, 'Feminist movement is not for you.'" Most importantly I knew firsthand that working for low wages did not liberate poor and working-class women from male domination.

When reformist feminist thinkers from privileged class backgrounds whose primary agenda was achieving social equality with men of their class equated work with liberation they meant high-paying careers. Their vision of work had little relevance for masses of women. Importantly the aspect of feminist emphasis on work which did affect all women was the demand for equal pay for equal work. Women gained more rights in relation to salaries and positions as a result of feminist protest but it has not completely eliminated gender discrimination. In many college classrooms today students both female and male will argue that feminist movement is no longer relevant since women now have equality. They do not even know that on the average most women still do not get equal pay for equal work, that we are more likely to make seventy-three cents for every dollar a male makes.

We know now that work does not liberate women from male domination. Indeed, there are many high-paid professional women, many rich women, who remain in relationships with men where male domination is the norm. Positively we do know that if a woman has access to economic self-sufficiency she is more likely to leave a relationship where male domination is the norm when she chooses liberation. She leaves because she can. Lots of women engage feminist thinking, choose liberation, but are economically tied to patriarchal males in ways that make leaving difficult if not downright impossible. Most women know now what some of us knew when the movement began, that work would not necessarily liberate us, but that this fact does not change the reality that economic self-sufficiency is needed if women are to be liberated. When we talk about economic self-sufficiency as liberating rather than work, we then have to take the next step and talk about what type of work liberates. Clearly better-paying jobs with comfortable time schedules tend to offer the greatest degree of freedom to the worker.

Masses of women feel angry because they were encouraged by feminist thinking to believe they would find liberation in the workforce. Mostly they have found that they work long hours at home and long hours at the job. Even before feminist movement encouraged women to feel positive about working outside the home, the needs of a depressed economy were already sanctioning this shift. If contemporary feminist movement had never taken place masses of women would still have entered the workforce, but it is unlikely that we would have the rights we have, had feminists not challenged gender discrimination. Women are wrong to "blame" feminism for making it so they have to work, which is what many women think. The truth remains that consumer capitalism was the force leading more women into the workforce. Given the depressed economy white middle-class families would be unable to sustain their class status and their lifestyles if women who had once dreamed solely of working as housewives had not chosen to work outside the home.

Feminist scholarship has documented that the positive benefits masses of women have gained by entering the workforce have more to do with increased self-esteem and positive participation in community. No matter her class the woman who stayed at home working as a housewife was often isolated, lonely, and depressed. While most workers do not feel secure at work, whether they are male or female, they do feel part of something larger than themselves. While problems at home cause greater stress and are difficult to solve, those in the workplace are shared by everyone, and the attempt to find solutions is not an isolated one. When men did most of the work women worked to make home a site of comfort and relaxation for males. Home was relaxing to women only when men and children were not present. When women in the home spend all their time attending to the needs of others, home is a workplace for her, not a site of relaxation, comfort, and pleasure. Work outside the home has been most liberating for women who are single (many of whom live alone; they may or may not be heterosexual). Most women have not even been able to find satisfying work, and their participation in the workforce has diminished the quality of their life at home.

Groups of highly educated privileged women previously unemployed or marginally employed were able through feminist changes in job discrimination to have greater access to work that satisfies, that serves as a base for economic self-sufficiency. Their success has not altered the fate of masses of women. Years ago in *Feminist Theory: From Margin to Center* I stated:

> If improving conditions in the workplace for women had been a central agenda for feminist movement in conjunction with efforts to obtain better-paying jobs for women and finding jobs for unemployed women of all classes, feminism would have been seen as a movement addressing the concerns of all women. Feminist focus on careerism, getting women employed in high-paying professions, not only alienated masses of women from feminist movement; it also allowed feminist activists to ignore the fact that increased entry of bourgeois women into the work force was not a sign that women as a group were gaining economic power. Had they looked at the economic situation of poor and working-class women, they would have seen the growing problem of unemployment and increased entry of women from all classes into the ranks of the poor.

Poverty has become a central woman's issue. White supremacist capitalist patriarchal attempts to dismantle the welfare system in our society will deprive poor and indigent women of access to even the most basic necessities of life: shelter and food. Indeed a return to patriarchal male-dominated households where men are providers is the solution offered women by conservative politicians who ignore the reality of mass unemployment for both women and men, and the fact that jobs simply are not there and that many men do not want to provide economically for women and children even if they have wages.

There is no feminist agenda in place offering women a way out — a way to rethink work. Since the cost of living in our society is high, work does not lead to economic self-sufficiency for most workers, women included. Yet economic self-sufficiency is needed if all women are to be free to choose against male domination, to be fully self-actualized.

The path to greater economic self-sufficiency will necessarily lead to alternative lifestyles which will run counter to the image of the good life presented to us by white supremacist capitalist patriarchal mass media. To live fully and well, to do work which enhances self-esteem and self-respect while being paid a living wage, we will need programs of job sharing. Teachers and service workers in all areas will need to be paid more. Women and men who want to stay home and raise children should have wages subsidized by the state as well as home-schooling programs that will enable them to finish high school and work on graduate degrees at home. With advanced technology individuals who remain home should be able to study by watching college courses on videos augmenting this with some period of time spent in classroom settings. If welfare not warfare (military spending) was sanctioned by our government and all citizens legally had access to a year or two of their lives during which they received state aid if they were unable to find a job, then the negative stigma attached to welfare programs would no longer exist. If men had equal access to welfare then it would no longer carry the stigma of gender.

A growing class divide separates masses of poor women from their privileged counterparts. Indeed much of the class power elite groups of women hold in our society, particularly those who are rich, is gained at the expense of the freedom of other women. Already there are small groups of women with class power working to build bridges through economic programs which provide aid and support to less privileged women. Individual wealthy women, particularly those with inherited wealth, who remain committed to feminist liberation are developing strategies for participatory economics which show their concern for and solidarity with women who lack class power. Right now these individuals are a small minority, but their ranks will swell as their work becomes more well known.

Thirty years ago contemporary feminists did not foresee the changes that would happen in the world of work in our society. They did not realize that mass unemployment would become more of a norm, that women could prepare themselves for jobs that would simply not be there. They did not foresee the conservative and sometimes liberal assault on welfare, the way that single mothers without money would be blamed for their economic plight and demonized. All these unforeseen realities require visionary feminist thinkers to think anew about the relationship between liberation and work.

While much feminist scholarship tells us about the role of women in the workforce today and how it changes their sense of self and their role in the home, we do not have many studies which tell us whether more women working has positively changed male domination. Many men blame women working for unemployment, for their loss of the stable identity being seen as patriarchal providers gave them, even if it was or is only a fiction. An important feminist agenda for the future has to be to realistically inform men about the nature of women and work so that they can see that women in the workforce are not their enemies.

Women have been in the workforce for a long time now. Whether we are paid well or receive low wages many women have not found work to be as meaningful as feminist utopian visions suggested. When women work to make money to consume more rather than to enhance the quality of our lives on all levels, work does not lead to economic self-sufficiency. More money does not mean more freedom if our finances are not used to facilitate well-being. Rethinking the meaning of work is an important task for future feminist movement. Addressing both ways women can leave the ranks of the poor as well as the strategies they can use to have a good life even if there is substantial material lack are vital to the success of feminist movement.

Early on feminist movement did not make economic self-sufficiency for women its primary goal. Yet addressing the economic plight of women may ultimately be the feminist platform that draws a collective response. It may well become the place of collective organizing, the common ground, the issue that unites all women.

10

RACE AND GENDER

No intervention changed the face of American feminism more than the demand that feminist thinkers acknowledge the reality of race and racism. All white women in this nation know that their status is different from that of black women/women of color. They know this from the time they are little girls watching television and seeing only their images, and looking at magazines and seeing only their images. They know that the only reason nonwhites are absent/invisible is because they are not white. All white women in this nation know that whiteness is a privileged category. The fact that white females may choose to repress or deny this knowledge does not mean they are ignorant: it means that they are in denial.

No group of white women understood the differences in their status and that of black women more than the group of politically conscious white females who were active in civil rights struggle. Diaries and memoirs of this period in American history written by white women document this knowledge. Yet many of these individuals moved from civil rights into women's liberation and spearheaded a feminist movement where they suppressed and denied the awareness of difference they had seen and heard articulated firsthand in civil rights struggle. Just because they participated in anti-racist struggle did not mean that they had divested of white supremacy, of notions that they were superior to black females, more informed, better educated, more suited to "lead" a movement.

In many ways they were following in the footsteps of their abolitionist ancestors who had demanded that everyone (white women and black people) be given the right to vote, but, when faced with the possibility that black males might gain the right to vote while they were denied it on the basis of gender, they chose to ally themselves with men, uniting under the rubric of white supremacy. Contemporary white females witnessing the militant demand for more rights for black people chose that moment to demand more rights for themselves. Some of these individuals claim that it was working on behalf of civil rights that made them aware of sexism and sexist oppression. Yet if this was the whole picture one might think their newfound political awareness of difference would have carried over into the way they theorized contemporary feminist movement.

They entered the movement erasing and denying difference, not playing race alongside gender, but eliminating race from the picture. Foregrounding gender meant that white women could take center stage, could claim the movement as theirs, even as they called on all women to join. The utopian vision of sisterhood evoked in a feminist movement that initially did not take racial difference or anti-racist struggle seriously did not capture the imagination of most black women/women of color. Individual black women who were active in the movement from its inception for the most part stayed in their place. When the feminist movement began racial integration was still rare. Many black people were learning how to interact with whites on the basis of being peers for the first time in their lives. No wonder individual black women choosing feminism were reluctant to introduce their awareness of race. It must have felt so awesome to have white women evoke sisterhood in a world where they had mainly experienced white women as exploiters and oppressors.

A younger generation of black females/women of color in the late '70s and early '80s challenged white female racism. Unlike our older black women allies we had for the most part been educated in predominantly white settings. Most of us had never been in a subordinated position in relation to a white female. Most of us had not been in the workforce. We had never been in our place. We were better positioned to critique racism and white supremacy within the women's movement. Individual white women who had attempted to organize the movement around the banner of common oppression evoking the notion that women constituted a sexual class/caste were the most reluctant to acknowledge differences among women, differences that overshadowed all the common experiences female shared. Race was the most obvious difference.

In the '70s I wrote the first draft of *Ain't I a Woman: Black Women and Feminism.* I was 19 years old. I had never worked a full-time job. I had come from a racially segregated small town in the south to Stanford University. While I had grown up resisting patriarchal thinking, college was the place where I embraced feminist politics. It was there as the only black female present in feminist classrooms, in consciousness-raising, that I began to engage race and gender theoretically. It was there that I began to demand recognition of the way in which racist biases were shaping feminist thinking and call for change. At other locations individual black women/women of color were making the same critique.

In those days white women who were unwilling to face the reality of racism and racial difference accused us of being traitors by introducing race. Wrongly they saw us as deflecting focus away from gender. In reality, we were demanding that we look at the status of females realistically, and that realistic understanding serve as the foundation for a real feminist politic. Our intent was not to diminish the vision of sisterhood. We sought to put in place a concrete politics of solidarity that would make genuine sisterhood possible. We knew that there could no real sisterhood between white women and women of color if white women were not able to divest of white supremacy, if feminist movement were not fundamentally anti-racist.

Critical interventions around race did not destroy the women's movement; it became stronger. Breaking through denial about race helped women face the reality of difference on all levels. And we were finally putting in place a movement that did not place the class interests of privileged women, especially white women, over that of all other women. We put in place a vision of sisterhood where all our realities could be spoken. There has been no contemporary movement for social justice where individual participants engaged in the dialectical exchange that occurred among feminist thinkers about race which led to the re-thinking of much feminist theory and practice. The fact that participants in the feminist movement could face critique and challenge while still remaining wholeheartedly committed to a vision of justice, of liberation, is a testament to the movement's strength and power. It shows us that no matter how misguided feminist thinkers have been in the past, the will to change, the will to create the context for struggle and liberation, remains stronger than the need to hold on to wrong beliefs and assumptions.

For years I witnessed the reluctance of white feminist thinkers to acknowledge the importance of race. I witnessed their refusal to divest of white supremacy, their unwillingness to acknowledge that an anti-racist feminist movement was the only political foundation that would make sisterhood be a reality. And I witnessed the revolution in consciousness that occurred as individual women began to break free of denial, to break free of white supremacist thinking. These awesome changes restore my faith in feminist movement and strengthen the solidarity I feel towards all women.

Overall feminist thinking and feminist theory has benefited

from all critical interventions on the issue of race. The only problematic arena has been that of translating theory into practice. While individual white women have incorporated an analysis of race into much feminist scholarship, these insights have not had as much impact on the day to day relations between white women and women of color. Anti-racist interactions between women are difficult in a society that remains racially segregated. Despite diverse work settings a vast majority of folks still socialize only with people of their own group. Racism and sexism combined create harmful barriers between women. So far feminist strategies to change this have not been very useful.

Individual white women and women of color who have worked through difficulties to make the space where bonds of love and political solidarity can emerge need to share the methods and strategies that we have successfully employed. Almost no attention is given the relationship between girls of different races. Biased feminist scholarship which attempts to show that white girls are somehow more vulnerable to sexist conditioning than girls of color simply perpetuates the white supremacist assumption that white females require and deserve more attention to their concerns and ills than other groups. Indeed while girls of color may express different behavior than their white counterparts they are not only internalizing sexist conditioning, they are far more likely to be victimized by sexism in ways that are irreparable.

Feminist movement, especially the work of visionary black activists, paved the way for a reconsideration of race and racism that has had positive impact on our society as a whole. Rarely do mainstream social critiques acknowledge this fact. As a feminist theorist who has written extensively about the issue of race and racism within feminist movement, I know that there remains much that needs to be challenged and changed, but it is equally important to celebrate the enormous changes that have occurred. That celebration, understanding our triumphs and using them as models, means that they can become the sound foundation for the building of a mass-based anti-racist feminist movement.

11

ENDING VIOLENCE

By far one of the most widespread positive interventions of contemporary feminist movement remains the effort to create and sustain greater cultural awareness of domestic violence as well as the changes that must happen in our thinking and action if we are to see its end. Nowadays the problem of domestic violence is talked about in so many circles, from mass media to grade schools, that it is often forgotten that contemporary feminist movement was the force that dramatically uncovered and exposed the ongoing reality of domestic violence. Initially feminist focus on domestic violence highlighted male violence against women, but as the movement progressed evidence showed that there was also domestic violence present in same-sex relations, that women in relationships with women were and are oftentimes the victims of abuse, that children were also victims of adult patriarchal violence enacted by women and men.

Patriarchal violence in the home is based on the belief that it is acceptable for a more powerful individual to control others through various forms of coercive force. This expanded definition of domestic violence includes male violence against women, same-sex violence, and adult violence against children. The term "patriarchal violence" is useful because unlike the more accepted phrase "domestic violence" it continually reminds the listener that violence in the home is connected to sexism and sexist thinking, to male domination. For too long the term domestic violence has been used as a "soft" term which suggests it emerges in an intimate context that is private and somehow less threatening, less brutal, than the violence that takes place outside the home. This is not so, since more women are beaten and murdered in the home than on the outside. Also most people tend to see domestic violence between adults as separate and distinct from violence against children when it is not. Often children suffer abuse as they attempt to protect a mother who is being attacked by a male companion or husband, or they are emotionally damaged by witnessing violence and abuse.

Just as a vast majority of citizens in this nation believe in equal pay for equal work most folks believe that men should not beat women and children. Yet when they are told that domestic violence is the direct outcome of sexism, that it will not end until sexism ends, they are unable to make this logical leap because it requires challenging and changing fundamental ways of thinking about gender. Significantly, I am among those rare feminist theorists who believe that it is crucial for feminist movement to have as an overriding agenda ending all forms of violence. Feminist focus on patriarchal violence against women should remain a primary concern. However emphasizing male violence against women in a manner which implies that it is more horrendous than all other forms of patriarchal violence does not serve to further the interests of feminist movement. It obscures the reality that much patriarchal violence is directed at children by sexist women and men.

In a zealous effort to call attention to male violence against women reformist feminist thinkers still choose often to portray females as always and only victims. The fact that many violent attacks on children are perpetrated by women is not equally highlighted and seen as another expression of patriarchal violence. We know now that children are violated not only when they are the direct targets of patriarchal violence but as well when they are forced to witness violent acts. Had all feminist thinkers expressed outrage at patriarchal violence perpetrated by women, placing it on an equal footing with male violence against women, it would have been and will be harder for the public to dismiss attention given patriarchal violence by seeing it as an anti-male agenda.

Adults who have been the victims of patriarchal violence perpetrated by females know that women are not nonviolent no matter the number of surveys that tell us women often are more inclined to use nonviolence. The truth is that children have no organized collective voice to speak the reality of how often they are the objects of female violence. Were it not for the huge numbers of children seeking medical attention because of violence done by women and men, there might be no evidence documenting female violence.

I first raised these concerns in the chapter "Feminist Movement to End Violence" in *Feminist Theory: From Margin to Center,* stating:

> It is essential for continued feminist struggle to end violence against women that this struggle be viewed as a component of an overall movement to end violence. So far feminist movement has primarily focused on male violence, and as a consequence lends credibility to sexist stereotypes that suggest men are violent, women are not; men are abusers, women are victims. This type of thinking allows us to ignore the extent to which women (with men) in this society accept and perpetuate the idea that it is acceptable for a dominant party or group to maintain power over the dominated by using coercive force. It allows us to overlook or ignore the extent to which women exert coercive authority over others or act violently. The fact that women may not commit violent acts as often as men does not negate the reality of female violence. We must see both men and women in this society as groups who support the use of violence if we are to eliminate it.

A mother who might never be violent but who teaches her children, especially her sons, that violence is an acceptable means of exerting social control, is still in collusion with patriarchal violence. Her thinking must be changed.

Clearly most women do not use violence to dominate men (even though small numbers of women batter the men in their lives) but lots of women believe that a person in authority has the right to use force to maintain authority. A huge majority of parents use some form of physical or verbal aggression against children. Since women remain the primary caretakers of children, the facts confirm the reality that given a hierarchal system in a culture of domination which empowers females (like the parent-child relationship) all too often they use coercive force to maintain dominance. In a culture of domination everyone is socialized to see violence as an acceptable means of social control. Dominant parties maintain power by the threat (acted upon or not) that abusive punishment, physical or psychological, will be used whenever the hierarchal structures in place are threatened, whether that be in male-female relationships, or parent and child bonds.

Male violence against women has received much ongoing media attention (highlighted by real-life court cases like the trial against O.J. Simpson) but awareness has not led the American public to challenge the underlying causes of this violence, to challenge patriarchy. Sexist thinking continues to support male domination and the violence that is a consequence. Since masses of unemployed and working-class men do not feel powerful on their jobs within white supremacist patriarchy they are encouraged to feel that the one place where they will have absolute authority and respect is in the home. Men are socialized by ruling-class groups of men to accept domination in the public world of work and to believe that the private world of home and intimate relationships will restore to them the sense of power they equate with masculinity. As more men have entered the ranks of the employed or receive low wages and more women have entered the world of work, some men feel that the use of violence is the only way they can establish and maintain power and dominance within the sexist sex role hierarchy. Until they unlearn the sexist thinking that tells them they have a right to rule over women by any means, male violence against women will continue to be a norm.

Early on in feminist thinking activists often failed to liken male violence against women to imperialist militarism. This linkage was often not made because those who were against male violence were often accepting and even supportive of militarism. As long as sexist thinking socializes boys to be "killers," whether in imaginary good guy, bad guy fights or as soldiers in imperialism to maintain coercive power over nations, patriarchal violence against women and children will continue. In recent years as young males from diverse class backgrounds have committed horrendous acts of violence there has been national condemnation of these acts but few attempts to link this violence to sexist thinking.

I conclude the chapter on violence in *Feminist Theory: From Margin to Center* emphasizing that men are not the only people who accept, condone, and perpetuate violence, who create a culture of violence. I urge women to take responsibility for the role women play in condoning violence:

> By only calling attention to male violence against women, or making militarism just another expression of male violence, we fail to adequately address the problem of violence and make it difficult to develop viable resistance strategies and solutions…. While we need not diminish the severity of the problem of male violence against women or male violence against nations or the planet, we must acknowledge that men and women have together made the United States a culture of violence and must work together to

transform and recreate that culture. Women and men must oppose the use of violence as a means of social control in all its manifestations: war, male violence against women, adult violence against children, teenage violence, racial violence, etc. Feminist efforts to end male violence against women must be expanded into a movement to end all forms of violence.

And it is especially vital that parents learn to parent in nonviolent ways. For our children will not turn away from violence if it is the only way they know to handle difficult situations.

In our nation masses of people are concerned about violence but resolutely refuse to link that violence to patriarchal thinking or male domination. Feminist thinking offers a solution. And it is up to us to make that solution available to everyone.

12

FEMINIST MASCULINITY

When contemporary feminist movement first began there was a fierce anti-male faction. Individual heterosexual women came to the movement from relationships where men were cruel, unkind, violent, unfaithful. Many of these men were radical thinkers who participated in movements for social justice, speaking out on behalf of the workers, the poor, speaking out on racial justice. But when it came to the issue of gender they were as sexist as their conservative cohorts. Individual women came from these relationships angry. And they used that anger as a catalyst for women's liberation. As the movement progressed, as feminist thinking advanced, enlightened feminist activists saw that men were not the problem, that the problem was patriarchy, sexism, and male domination. It was difficult to face the reality that the problem did not just lie with men. Facing that reality required more complex theorizing; it required acknowledging the role women play in maintaining and perpetuating sexism. As more women moved away from destructive relationships with men it was easier to see the whole picture. It became evident that even if individual men divested of patriarchal privilege the system of patriarchy, sexism, and male domination would still remain intact, and women would still be exploited and/or oppressed.

Conservative mass media constantly represented feminist women

as man-haters. And when there was an anti-male faction or sentiment in the movement, they highlighted it as a way of discrediting
feminism. Embedded in the portrayal of feminists as man-hating
was the assumption that all feminists were lesbians. Appealing to
homophobia, mass media intensified anti-feminist sentiment
among men. Before contemporary feminist movement was less
than 10 years old, feminist thinkers began to talk about the way in
which patriarchy was harmful to men. Without changing our fierce
critique of male domination feminist politics expanded to include
the recognition that patriarchy stripped men of certain rights, imposing on them a sexist masculine identity.

Anti-feminist men have always had a strong public voice. The
men who feared and hated feminist thinking and feminist activists
were quick to marshal their collective forces and attack the movement. But from the onset of the movement there was a small group
of men who recognized that feminist movement was as valid a
movement for social justice as all the other radical movements in
our nation's history that men had supported. These men became
our comrades in our struggle and our allies. Individual heterosexual
women active in the movement were often in intimate relationships
with the men who were struggling to come to terms with feminism.
Their conversion to feminist thinking was often a matter of rising to
meet the challenge or risking the termination of intimate bonds.

Anti-male factions within the feminist movement resented the
presence of anti-sexist men because their presence served to counter any insistence that all men are oppressors, or that all men hate
women. It promoted the interests of feminist women who were
seeking greater class mobility and access to forms of patriarchal
power to polarize men and women by putting us in neat categories
of oppressor/oppressed. They portrayed all men as the enemy in order to represent all women as victims. This focus on men deflected

attention from the class privilege of individual feminist activists as well as their desire to increase their class power. Those individual activists who called on all women to reject men refused to look at either the caring bonds women shared with men or the economic and emotional ties (however positive or negative) that bind women to men who are sexist.

Feminists who called for a recognition of men as comrades in struggle never received mass media attention. Our theoretical work critiquing the demonization of men as the enemy did not change the perspectives of women who were anti-male. And it was reaction to negative representations of manhood that led to the development of a men's movement that was anti-female. Writing about the "men's liberation movement" I called attention to the opportunism undergirding this movement:

> These men identified themselves as victims of sexism, working to liberate men. They identified rigid sex roles as the primary source of their victimization, and, though they wanted to change the notion of masculinity, they were not particularly concerned with their sexist exploitation and oppression of women.

In many ways the men's movement mirrored the most negative aspects of the women's movement.

Even though anti-male factions within feminist movement were small in number it has been difficult to change the image of feminist women as man-hating in the public imagination. Of course by characterizing feminism as being man-hating males could deflect attention away from the accountability for male domination. If feminist theory had offered more liberatory visions of masculinity it would have been impossible for anyone to dismiss the movement as anti-male. To a grave extent feminist movement failed to attract a large body of females and males because our theory did not effectively address the issue of not just what males might do to be anti-sexist but also what an alternative masculinity might look like. Often the only alternative to patriarchal masculinity presented by feminist movement or the men's movement was a vision of men becoming more "feminine." The idea of the feminine that was evoked emerged from sexist thinking and did not represent an alternative to it.

What is and was needed is a vision of masculinity where self-esteem and self-love of one's unique being forms the basis of identity. Cultures of domination attack self-esteem, replacing it with a notion that we derive our sense of being from dominion over another. Patriarchal masculinity teaches men that their sense of self and identity, their reason for being, resides in their capacity to dominate others. To change this males must critique and challenge male domination of the planet, of less powerful men, of women and children. But they must also have a clear vision of what feminist masculinity looks like. How can you become what you cannot imagine? And that vision has yet to be made fully clear by feminist thinkers male or female.

As is often the case in revolutionary movements for social justice we are better at naming the problem than we are at envisioning the solution. We do know that patriarchal masculinity encourages men to be pathologically narcissistic, infantile, and psychologically dependent on the privileges (however relative) that they receive simply for having been born male. Many men feel that their lives are being threatened if these privileges are taken away, as they have structured no meaningful core identity. That is why the men's movement positively attempted to teach men how to reconnect with their feelings, to reclaim the lost boy within and nurture his soul, his spiritual growth.

No significant body of feminist literature has appeared that addresses boys, that lets them know how they can construct an identity that is not rooted in sexism. Anti-sexist men have done little education for critical consciousness which includes a focus on boyhood, especially the development of adolescent males. As a consequence of this gap, now that discussions about the raising of boys are receiving national attention, feminist perspectives are rarely if ever part of the discussion. Tragically, we are witnessing a resurgence of harmful misogynist assumptions that mothers cannot raise healthy sons, that boys "benefit" from patriarchal militaristic notions of masculinity which emphasize discipline and obedience to authority. Boys need healthy self-esteem. They need love. And a wise and loving feminist politics can provide the only foundation to save the lives of male children. Patriarchy will not heal them. If that were so they would all be well.

Most men in this nation feel troubled about the nature of their identity. Even though they cling to patriarchy they are beginning to intuit that it is part of the problem. Lack of jobs, the unrewarding nature of paid labor, and the increased class power of women, has made it difficult for men who are not rich and powerful to know where they stand. White supremacist capitalist patriarchy is not able to provide all it has promised. Many men are anguished because they do not engage the liberating critiques that could enable them to face that these promises were rooted in injustice and domination and even when fulfilled have never led men to glory. Bashing liberation while reinscribing the white supremacist capitalist patriarchal ways of thinking that have murdered their souls in the first place, they are just as lost as many boys.

A feminist vision which embraces feminist masculinity, which loves boys and men and demands on their behalf every right that we desire for girls and women, can renew the American male. Feminist thinking teaches us all, especially, how to love justice and freedom in ways that foster and affirm life. Clearly we need new strategies, new theories, guides that will show us how to create a world where feminist masculinity thrives.

13

FEMINIST PARENTING

Feminist focus on children was a central component of contemporary radical feminist movement. By raising children without sexism women hoped to create a future world where there would be no need for an anti-sexist movement. Initially the focus on children primarily highlighted sexist sex roles and the way in which they were imposed on children from birth on. Feminist attention to children almost always focused on girl children, on attacking sexist biases and promoting alternative images. Now and then feminists would call attention to the need to raise boys in an anti-sexist manner but for the most part the critique of male patriarchy, the insistence that all men had it better than all women, trickled down. The assumption that boys always had more privilege and power than girls fueled feminists prioritizing a focus on girls.

One of the primary difficulties feminist thinkers faced when confronting sexism within families was that more often than not female parents were the transmitters of sexist thinking. Even in households where no adult male parental caregiver was present, women taught and teach children sexist thinking. Ironically, many people assume that any female-headed household is automatically matriarchal. In actuality women who head households in patriarchal society often feel guilty about the absence of a male figure and are hypervigilant about imparting sexist values to children, especially males. In recent times mainstream conservative pundits have responded to a wellspring of violent acts by young males of all classes and races by suggesting that single women cannot possible raise a healthy male child. This is just simply not true. The facts show that some of the most loving and powerful men in our society were raised by single mothers. Again it must be reiterated that most people assume that a woman raising children alone, especially sons, will fail to teach a male child how to become a patriarchal male. This is simply not the case.

Within white supremacist capitalist patriarchal cultures of domination children do not have rights. Feminist movement was the first movement for social justice in this society to call attention to the fact that ours is a culture that does not love children, that continues to see children as the property of parents to do with as they will. Adult violence against children is a norm in our society. Problematically, for the most part feminist thinkers have never wanted to call attention to the reality that women are often the primary culprits in everyday violence against children simply because they are the primary parental caregivers. While it was crucial and revolutionary that feminist movement called attention to the fact that male domination in the home often creates an autocracy where men sexually abuse children, the fact is that masses of children are daily abused verbally and physically by women and men. Maternal sadism often leads women to emotionally abuse children, and feminist theory has not yet offered both feminist critique and feminist intervention when the issue is adult female violence against children.

In a culture of domination where children have no civil rights, those who are powerful, adult males and females, can exert autocratic rule of children. All the medical facts show that children are violently abused daily in this society. Much of that abuse is life-threatening. Many children die. Women perpetuate this violence as much as men if not more. A serious gap in feminist thinking and practice has been the refusal of the movement to confront head-on adult female violence against children. Emphasizing male domination makes it easy for women, including feminist thinkers, to ignore the ways women abuse children because we have all been socialized to embrace patriarchal thinking, to embrace an ethics of domination which says the powerful have the right to rule over the powerless and can use any means to subordinate them. In the hierarchies of white supremacist capitalist patriarchy, male domination of females is condoned, but so is adult domination of children. And no one really wants to call attention to mothers who abuse.

Often I tell the story of being at a fancy dinner party where a woman is describing the way she disciplines her young son by pinching him hard, clamping down on his little flesh for as long as it takes to control him. And how everyone applauded her willingness to be a disciplinarian. I shared the awareness that her behavior was abusive, that she was potentially planting the seeds for this male child to grow up and be abusive to women. Significantly, I told the audience of listeners that if we had heard a man telling us how he just clamps down on a woman's flesh, pinching her hard to control her behavior it would have been immediately acknowledged as abusive. Yet when a child is being hurt this form of negative domination is condoned. This is not an isolated incident — much more severe violence against children is enacted daily by mothers and fathers.

Indeed the crisis the children of this nation face is that patriarchal thinking clashing with feminist changes is making the family even more of a war zone than it was when male domination was the norm in every household. Feminist movement served as the catalyst, uncovering and revealing the grave extent to which male sexual abuse of children has been and is taking place in the patriarchal family. It started with grown women in feminist movement receiving therapeutic care acknowledging that they were abuse survivors and bringing this acknowledgment out of the private realm of therapy into public discourse. These revelations created the positive ethical and moral context for children to confront abuse taking place in the present. However, simply calling attention to male sexual abuse of children has not created the climate where masses of people understand that this abuse is linked to male domination, that it will end only when patriarchy is eliminated. Male sexual abuse of children happens more often and is reported more often than female abuse, but female sexual coercion of children must be seen as just as horrendous as male abuse. And feminist movement must critique women who abuse as harshly as we critique male abuse. Beyond the realm of sexual abuse, violence against children takes many forms; the most commonplace forms are acts of verbal and psychological abuse.

Abusive shaming lays the foundation for other forms of abuse. Male children are often subjected to abuse when their behavior does not conform to sexist notions of masculinity. They are often shamed by sexist adults (particularly mothers) and other children. When male parental caregivers embody anti-sexist thought and behavior boys and girls have the opportunity to see feminism in action. When feminist thinkers and activists provide children with educational arenas where anti-sexist biases are not the standards used to judge behavior, boys and girls are able to develop healthy self-esteem.

One of the most positive interventions feminist movement made on behalf of children was to create greater cultural awareness of the need for men to participate equally in parenting not just to create gender equity but to build better relationships with children. Future feminist studies will document all the ways anti-sexist male parenting enhances the lives of children. Concurrently, we need to know more about feminist parenting in general, about the practical ways one can raise a child in an anti-sexist environment, and most importantly we need to know more about what type of people the children who are raised in these homes become.

Visionary feminist activists have never denied the importance and value of male parental caregivers even as we continually work to create greater cultural appreciation of motherhood and the work done by women who mother. A disservice is done to all females when praise for male participation in parenting leads to disparagement and devaluation of the positive job of mothering women do. At the beginning of feminist movement feminists were harsh critics of mothering, pitting that task against careers which were deemed more liberating, more self-affirming. However, as early as the mid-'80s some feminist thinkers were challenging feminist devaluation of motherhood and the overvaluation of work outside the home. Writing on this subject in *Feminist Theory: From Margin to Center* I made the point that:

> Working within a social context where sexism is still the norm, where there is unnecessary competition promoting envy, distrust, antagonism, and malice between individuals, makes work stressful, frustrating, and often totally unsatisfying...many women who like and enjoy the wage work they do feel that it takes too much of their time, leaving little space for other satisfying pursuits. While work may help women gain a degree of financial independence or even financial self-sufficiency, for most women it has not adequately fulfilled human needs. As a consequence women's search for fulfilling labor done in an environment of care has led to reemphasizing the importance of family and the positive aspects of motherhood.

Ironically just when feminist thinkers had worked to create a more balanced portrait of mothering patriarchal mainstream culture launched a vicious critique of single-parent, female-headed households. That critique was most harsh when it came to the question of welfare. Ignoring all the data which shows how skillfully loving single mothers parent with very little income whether they receive state assistance or work for a wage, patriarchal critiques call attention to dysfunctional female-headed households, act as though these are the norm, then suggest the problem can be solved if men were in the picture as patriarchal providers and heads of households.

No anti-feminist backlash has been as detrimental to the well-being of children as societal disparagement of single mothers. In a culture which holds the two-parent patriarchal family in higher esteem than any other arrangement, all children feel emotionally insecure when their family does not measure up to the standard. A utopian vision of the patriarchal family remains intact despite all the evidence which proves that the well-being of children is no more secure in the dysfunctional male-headed household than in the dysfunctional female-headed household. Children need to be raised in loving environments. Whenever domination is present love is lacking. Loving parents, be they single or coupled, gay or straight, headed by females or males, are more likely to raise healthy, happy children with sound self-esteem. In future feminist movement we need to work harder to show parents the ways ending sexism positively changes family life. Feminist movement is pro-family. Ending patriarchal domination of children, by men or women, is the only way to make the family a place where children can be safe, where they can be free, where they can know love.

14

LIBERATING MARRIAGE AND PARTNERSHIP

When contemporary feminist movement was at its peak the institution of marriage was harshly critiqued. The entrance of many heterosexual women into the movement had been sparked by male domination in intimate relationships, particularly long-time marriages where gender inequity was the norm. From the onset the movement challenged the double standard in relationship to sexuality which condemned females who were not virgins or faithful lovers and spouses while allowing men the space to do whatever they desired sexually and have their behavior condoned. The sexual liberation movement strengthened feminist critique of marriage, especially the demand for safe, affordable birth control.

Early on feminist activists focused so much attention on private bonds and domestic relationships because it was in those circumstances that women of all classes and races felt the brunt of male domination, whether from patriarchal parents or spouses. A woman might assertively challenge a sexist male boss or stranger's attempt to dominate her, then go home and submit to her partner. Contemporary feminists, both those heterosexual women who had come from long-time marriages and lesbian allies in struggle, critiqued marriage as yet another form of sexual slavery. They highlighted the way traditionally sexist bonds led to marriages where elements of intimacy, care, and respect were sacrificed so that men could be on top — could be patriarchs ruling the roost.

Early on many feminist women were pessimistic about men changing. Some heterosexual women decided that they would choose celibacy or lesbianism over seeking after unequal relationships with sexist men. Others saw sexual monogamy with men as reinforcing the idea that the female body was property belonging to the individual male she was bonded with. We chose non-monogamous relationships and often refused to marry. We believed living with a male partner without state-sanctioned marriage within patriarchal society helped men maintain a healthy respect for female autonomy. Feminists advocated demanding an end to sexual slavery and called attention to the prevalence of marital rape while at the same time championing the rights of women to express sexual desire, initiate sexual interaction, and be sexually fulfilled.

There were many heterosexual men who embraced feminist thinking precisely because they were unfulfilled sexually in relationships with partners who were not interested in sex because they had been taught virtuous women were not sexually active. These men were grateful to feminist movement for offering a liberatory sexual paradigm for female mates because it ensured that they would have a more fulfilling sex life. By challenging the notion that a woman's virtue was determined by her sexual practice feminist thinkers not only took away the stigma attached to not being a virgin; they placed female sexual well-being on a equal par with that of men. Urging women to no longer pretend that they were sexually fulfilled when this was not the case, feminist movement threatened to expose male sexual shortcomings.

To defuse this threat sexist men continually insisted that most feminists were lesbians or that all any feminist woman needed was "a good fuck" to put her back in her place. In actuality feminist rebellion exposed the fact that many women were not having satisfying sex with men in patriarchal relationships. In relationship to intimate bonds most men were more willing to embrace feminist changes in female sexuality which led women to be more sexually active than those changes which demanded of men a change in their sexual behavior. The absence of sexual foreplay was a much discussed issue when feminist agendas first focused on heterosexuality. Straight women were tired of male sexual coercion and lack of concern with female pleasure. Feminist focus on sexual pleasure gave women the language to critique and challenge male sexual behavior.

When it came to sexual freedom women made great strides. The critique of monogamy has been forgotten as the prevalence of sexually transmitted diseases has made it more difficult for females to choose sexual promiscuity. The prevalence of life-threatening diseases like AIDS, which tend to be more easily transmitted male to female, in a patriarchal culture where men are encouraged to lie to women, have made it harder for heterosexual women to choose a variety of partners. Clearly, when the emphasis is on monogamy in heterosexual bonds within patriarchy it is often harder for couples to break with sexist paradigms. Concurrently within patriarchy many individual feminist women found that non-monogamous relationships often simply gave men more power while undermining women. While women will freely choose to have sex with a man who is partnered with another woman, men will often show no sexual interest in a woman who is partnered. Or they will continually concede power to the male the woman is partnered with, even going so far as to seek his approval of their involvement. Despite these difficulties, women having the freedom to be non-monogamous, whether we exercise that freedom or not, continues to disrupt and challenge the notion that the female body belongs to men. Like all the positive changes produced by feminist critique of sexist notions of sexual pleasure it has helped create a world where women and men can have more satisfying sexual relationships.

At first it appeared that changes in the nature of sexual bonds would lead to other changes in domestic relationships, that men would also do an equal share of household chores and child care. Nowadays so many males acknowledge that they should do household chores, whether they actually do them or not, that young women see no need to make sharing chores an issue; they just accept this as a norm. Of course the reality is that it has never become the norm, that for the most part women still do most of the housework and child care. Overall men were more willing to accept and affirm equality in the bedroom than to accept equality around housework and child care. Not surprisingly, as individual women gained in class power many women deal with inequity by hiring caretakers to do the tasks neither they nor male partners want to perform. Yet when a heterosexual couple pays help to do the tasks sexist thinking defines as "female" it is usually the woman who employs the help and oversees this work.

More than any factor the feminist critique of mothering as the sole satisfying purpose of a woman's life changed the nature of marriage and long-time partnerships. Once a woman's worth was no longer determined by whether or not she birthed and raised children it was possible for a two-career couple who wanted to remain childless to envision a peer marriage — a relationship between equals. The absence of children made it easier to be peers simply because the way in which patriarchal society automatically assumes certain tasks will be done by mothers almost always makes it harder for women to achieve gender equity around child care. For example: it is very telling that in the wake of feminist movement the patriarchal medical establishment which had previously downplayed breast-feeding suddenly began to be not only positive about breast-feeding, but insistent. This is just one aspect of child-rearing that automatically places more responsibility on the birthing female whether she is heterosexual or lesbian. Certainly many women in relationships with males often found that having a newborn baby plummeted their relationships back into more sexist-defined roles. However when couples work hard to maintain equity in all spheres, especially child care, it can be the reality; the key issue, though, is working hard. And most men have not chosen to work hard at child care.

Positively feminist interventions called attention to the value and importance of male parenting both in regards to the well-being of children and gender equity. When males participate equally in parenting, relationships between women and men are better, whether the two parents are married or live together or separately. Because of feminist movement more men do more parenting than ever before, yet we have not achieved even a semblance of gender equity. And we know that this equal participation makes parenting a more positive and fulfilling experience for all parties involved. Of course the demands of work often create the obstacles to more participation in child care by working parents, especially men. Until we see major changes in the way work is structured timewise, we will not live in a world where life is designed to allow men the time and space to parent. In that world men might be more eager to parent. But until then, many working males who are overtired and underpaid will all too willingly accept a woman doing all the child care, even if she is overtired and underpaid. The world of work within white supremacist capitalist patriarchy has made it harder for women to parent fully. Indeed, this reality is leading women who might choose a career to stay home. Rather than sexist thinking about male domination becoming the factor which takes women out of the workforce and puts them back in the home, it is the fear that we are raising a society of "parentless" children. Many women find competitive careerism leaves little time for nurturing loving relationships. The fact that no one talks about men leaving work to be full-time parents shows the extent to which sexist thinking about roles prevails. Most people in our society still believe women are better at raising children than men.

To a grave extent women, who on one hand critiqued motherhood but on the other hand also enjoyed the special status and privileges it gave them, especially when it came to parent-child bonding, were not as willing to relinquish pride of place in parenting to men as feminist thinkers hoped. Individual feminist thinkers who critiqued biological determinism in every other area often embraced it when it came to the issue of mothering. They were not able to fully embrace the notion that fathers are just as important as mothers, and can parent just as well. These contradictions, along with the predominance of sexist thinking, have undermined the feminist demand for gender equity when it comes to child care.

Nowadays mass media continually bombards us with the message that marriage has made a comeback. Marriage never went out of fashion. Often when people proclaim that it is making a comeback, what they really mean is that more sexist-defined notions of marriage are "in" again. This fact is troubling to feminist movement because it is just as clear today as it was yesterday that marriages built on a sexist foundation are likely to be deeply troubled and rarely last. Traditionally sexist marriages are more and more in vogue. And while they tend to breed the seeds of misery and dissatisfaction that served as a catalyst for feminist rebellion in domestic relationships, the factor that breaks with tradition is that these bonds are often severed quickly. Folks marry young and divorce young.

Patriarchal male domination in marriage and partnerships has been the primary force creating breakups and divorces in our society. All recent studies of successful marriages show that gender equity creates a context where each member of the couple is likely to be affirmed. This affirmation creates greater happiness, and, even if the marriage does not last forever, the peer friendship that has been the foundation of the bond continues. Significantly, in future feminist movement we will spend less time critiquing patriarchal marriage bonds and expend more effort showing alternatives, showing the value of peer relationships which are founded on principles of equality, respect, and the belief that mutual satisfaction and growth are needed for partnerships to be fulfilling and lasting.

15

A FEMINIST SEXUAL POLITIC
An Ethics of Mutual Freedom

Before feminist movement, before sexual liberation, most women found it difficult, if not downright impossible, to assert healthy sexual agency. Sexist thinking taught to females from birth on had made it clear that the domain of sexual desire and sexual pleasure was always and only male, that only a female of little or no virtue would lay claim to sexual need or sexual hunger. Divided by sexist thinking into the roles of madonnas or whores females had no basis on which to construct a healthy sexual self. Luckily feminist movement immediately challenged sexist sexual stereotypes. It helped that this challenge came at a time in our nation's history where dependable birth control was made accessible to all.

Before dependable birth control female sexual self-assertion could lead always to the "punishment" of unwanted pregnancy and the dangers of illegal abortion. We have not amassed enough testimony to let the world know the sexual pathologies and horrors women endured prior to the existence of dependable birth control. It evokes fear within me just to imagine a world where every time a female is sexual she risks being impregnated, to imagine a world where men want sex and women fear it. In such world a desiring woman might find the intersection of her desire and her fear. We have not amassed enough testimony telling us what women did to ward off male sexual advances, how they coped with ongoing marital rape, how they coped with risking death to deal with unwanted pregnancies. We do know that the world of female sexuality was forever changed by the coming of feminist sexual revolution.

For those of us who had witnessed the sexual pain and bitterness of our mothers, their out-and-out fear and hatred of sexuality, coming into a movement, just as we were becoming more sexual, that promised us freedom, pleasure, and delight was awesome. Nowadays females face so few obstacles inhibiting their expression of sexual desire that our culture risks burying the historical memory of patriarchal assault on women's bodies and sexuality. In that place of forgetfulness efforts to make abortion illegal can focus on the issue of whether or not a life is being taken without ever bringing into the discussion the devastating effects ending legal abortion would have on female sexuality. We still live among generations of women who have never known sexual pleasure, women for whom sex has only ever meant loss, threat, danger, annihilation.

Female sexual freedom requires dependable, safe birth control. Without it females cannot exercise full control of the outcome of sexual activity. But female sexual freedom also requires knowledge of one's body, an understanding of the meaning of sexual integrity. Early feminist activism around sexuality focused so much attention on just the politics of granting females the right to be sexual whenever we wanted to be, with whomever we wanted to be sexual with, that there was little feminist education for critical consciousness teaching us how to respect our bodies in an anti-sexist way, teaching us what liberatory sex might look like.

In the late '60s and early '70s females were often encouraged to make synonymous sexual freedom and sexual promiscuity. In those days and to some extent in the present most heterosexual men saw and see a sexually liberated female as the one who would be or will be sexual with the least amount of fuss, i.e., asserting no demands, particularly emotional ones. And a large number of heterosexual feminists had the same misguided notions because they were patterning their behavior on the model provided by patriarchal males. However it did not take women long to realize that sexual promiscuity and sexual liberation were not one and the same.

When feminist movement was "hot" radical lesbian activists constantly demanded that straight women reconsider their bonds with men, raising the question of whether or not it was possible for women to ever have a liberated heterosexual experience within a patriarchal context. This interrogation was useful for the movement. It not only forced straight women to engage in ongoing critical vigilance about heterosexual practice, it highlighted lesbians in ways that positively exposed their strength while also revealing weaknesses. Individual women who moved from having relationships with men to choosing women because they were seduced by the popular slogan "feminism is the theory, lesbianism the practice" soon found that these relationships were as emotionally demanding and as fraught with difficulties as any other.

The degree to which lesbian partnership was as good as or better than heterosexual bonds was usually determined not by both parties being of the same sex but by the extent of their commitment to breaking with notions of romance and partnership informed by a culture of domination's sadomasochistic assumption that in every relationship there is a dominant and a submissive party. Sexual promiscuity among lesbians could no more be equated with sexual liberation than it could be in heterosexual practice. Irrespective of their sexual preference women who suffered emotionally by equating the two were disillusioned about sex. And given the connection between male domination and sexual violence it is not surprising that women who had been involved with men were often the most vocal about their sexual unhappiness.

The consequence of this disillusionment with the dream of sexual freedom was that many individual feminist thinkers either came away from coping with these experiences, and/or the negative fallout a female friend or comrade faced, harboring repressed resentment about all sexual activity, especially sexual contact with men. Radical lesbians who had once been the lone voices calling women to account for "sleeping with the enemy" were now joined by heterosexual women who were choosing same-sex bonds because they were utterly disillusioned with men. Suddenly the discourse on sexuality, particularly all discussion of intercourse, that emerged made it seem that all coitus was sexual coercion, that any penetration of the female by the male was rape. For a time these theories and the individual charismatic women who spread the news had a deep impact on the consciousness of young women who were struggling to establish new and different sexual identities. Many of these young women ended up choosing bisexual practice or choosing relationships with men where it was agreed that the female partner would determine the nature of all sexual encounter. However masses of young females simply turned away from feminist thinking. And in this turning found their way back to outmoded sexist notions of sexual freedom and embraced them, at times with a vengeance.

No wonder then that the contradictions and conflicts arising as a consequence of the tensions between sexual pleasure and danger, sexual freedom and bondage, provided the seductive proving ground for sexual sadomasochism. Ultimately feminist interrogations of sexuality were all tied to a question of power. No matter how much feminist thinkers talked about equality, when it came to sexual desire and the enactment of sexual passion the dynamics of power and powerlessness evoked in the sexual arena disrupted simplistic notions of oppressor and oppressed. Nothing challenged the grounds of feminist critique of heterosexual practice more than the revelation that feminist lesbians engaged in sexual sadomasochism, a world of tops and bottoms, wherein positions of powerful and powerless were deemed acceptable.

Practically all radical feminist discussion of sexuality ceased when women within the movement began to fight over the issue of whether or not one could be a liberated woman, whether lesbian or heterosexual, and engage in the practice of sexual sadomasochism. Tied to this issue were differences of opinion about the meaning and significance of patriarchal pornography. Faced with issues powerful enough to divide and disrupt the movement, by the late '80s most radical feminist dialogues about sexuality were no longer public; they took place privately. Talking about sexuality publicly had devastated the movement.

Publicly the feminist women who continued to talk the most about sexuality tended to be conservative, at times puritanical and anti-sex. The movement had been radically changed, moving from being a site where female sexual liberation had been called for and celebrated to a site where public discussions of sexuality focused more on sexual violence and victimization. Mainstream aging feminist individual women who had once been the great champions of female sexual freedom for the most part began to talk about sexual pleasure as unimportant, valorizing celibacy. Increasingly women who speak and write openly about sexual desire and practice tend to dismiss or distance themselves from feminist sexual politics. And more than ever the feminist movement is seen primarily as anti-sex. Visionary feminist discourse on sexual passion and pleasure has been pushed into the background, ignored by almost everyone. In its place females and males continue to rely on patriarchal models of sexual freedom.

Despite sexual revolution and feminist movement we know that many heterosexual females have sex only because males want them to, that young homosexuals, male and female, still have no public or private supportive environment that affirms their sexual preference, that the sexist iconography of madonna or whore continues to claim the erotic imagination of males and females, that patriarchal pornography now permeates every aspect of mass media, that unwanted pregnancy is on the increase, that teens are having often unsatisfying and unsafe sex, that in many long-time marriages and partnerships, whether same-sex or heterosexual, women are having no sex. All these facts call attention to the need for renewed feminist dialogue about sexuality. We still need to know what liberatory sexual practice looks like.

Fundamentally mutual respect is essential to liberatory sexual practice and the conviction that sexual pleasure and fulfilment is best attained in a circumstance of choice and consensual agreement. Within patriarchal society men and women cannot know sustained heterosexual bliss unless both parties have divested of their sexist thinking. Many women and men still consider male sexual performance to be determined solely by whether or not the penis is hard and erections are maintained. This notion of male performance is tied to sexist thinking. While men must let go of the sexist assumption that female sexuality exists to serve and satisfy their needs, many women must also let go a fixation on penetration.

During the heyday of sexual liberation and contemporary feminist movement women found that men were often willing to accept equality in every sphere except sexuality. In the bedroom many men want a sexually desiring woman eager to give and share pleasure but ultimately they did not surrender the sexist assumption that her sexual performance (i.e., whether or not she wanted to be sexual) should be determined by their desire. While it was fun to do it with willing excited, liberated females it was not fun when those females declared that they wanted a space not to be sexual. Often when that happened heterosexual men made it clear that they would need to took elsewhere for sexual release, an action which reinforced the reality of continued allegiance to a sexist paradigm of ownership in the female body as well as their holding to the notion that any female body would suffice. In a liberatory heterosexual or homosexual relationships both parties should be free to determine when and how frequently they want to be sexual without fear of punishment. Until all men cease to believe that someone other than themselves is required to respond to their sexual needs demanding sexual subordination of partners will continue.

A truly liberatory feminist sexual politic will always make the assertion of female sexual agency central. That agency cannot come into being when females believe their sexual bodies must always stand in the service of something else. Often professional prostitutes and women in everyday life hold up their free exchange of pussy for goods or services as an indication that they are liberated. They refuse to acknowledge the fact that whenever a woman prostitutes her body because she cannot satisfy material needs in other ways she risks forfeiting that space of sexual integrity where she controls her body.

Masses of heterosexual women remain unable to let go the sexist assumption that their sexuality must always be sought after by men to have meaning and value. To do so they must believe that same-sex sexual encounters, self-pleasuring, and celibacy are as vital and life-enhancing as sexual intercourse with men within patriarchal culture. Aging females, many of whom once advocated feminist change, often find that they must subscribe to sexist notions of femininity and sexual desirability in order to have any sexual contact with men whom they fear will trade them in for a younger model. To some extent then radical feminist thinkers were right years ago when they suggested that women would only be truly sexually liberated when we arrived at a place where we could see ourselves as having sexual value and agency irrespective of whether or not we were the objects of male desire. Again we need feminist theory to show us how this sexual feeling and identity expresses itself within the context of a society that remains deeply patriarchal.

Despite the limitations of feminist discourse on sexuality, feminist politics still is the only movement for social justice that offers a vision of mutual well-being as a consequence of its theory and practice. We need an erotics of being that is founded on the principle that we have a right to express sexual desire as the spirit moves us and to find in sexual pleasure a life-affirming ethos. Erotic connection calls us away from isolation and alienation into community. In a world where positive expressions of sexual longing connect us we will all be free to choose those sexual practices which affirm and nurture our growth. Those practices may range from choosing promiscuity or celibacy, from embracing one specific sexual identity and preference or choosing a roaming uncharted desire that is kindled only by interaction and engagement with specific individuals with whom we feel the spark of erotic recognition no matter their sex, race, class, or even their sexual preference. Radical feminist dialogues about sexuality must surface so that the movement towards sexual freedom can begin again.

16

TOTAL BLISS
Lesbianism and Feminism

Sometimes it's hard to know which came first, the movement for women's liberation or sexual liberation — for some activists they happened at the same time, blending into one another. This was certainly true for many of the bisexual and lesbian women who were part of the first contemporary feminist vanguard. These women were not led to feminism because they were lesbian. Masses of lesbians were not "into" politics, were conservative, and had no desire to do anything radical. The lesbians and bisexual women who helped form the women's liberation vanguard were led to feminism because they were already engaged in left politics, pushing against fixed boundaries of class, race, and sexuality. Women's liberation had already been an issue they had claimed psychologically, rebelling against traditional notions of gender and desire.

Simply being lesbian does not make one a feminist, anymore than being lesbian makes one political. Being a member of an exploited group does not make anyone more inclined to resist. If it did, all women (and that includes every lesbian on the planet) would have wanted to participate in the women's movement. Experience coupled with awareness and choice are the factors that usually lead women into leftist politics. Having done so much of the menial tasks as well as the behind the scenes radical thinking in socialist circles and in the civil rights and militant black power movements, individual radical women from various walks of life were ready to get justice for themselves; they were ready for feminist movement. And among the most ready, the truly visionary and courageous, were and are many lesbian women.

I came to feminism before I had my first sexual experience. I was a teenager. Before I knew anything about women's rights I knew about homosexuality. In the narrowminded world of southern religious fundamentalism, of racial apartheid, in our black community gay people were known and often had special status; often they were men with class power. Homosexuality among men was more accepted than lesbianism. The lesbians in our small, segregated black community were usually married. Yet they knew who they really were. And they let their real selves be known behind closed doors, at secret jook joints and parties. One of the women accused of being lesbian chose to mentor me; a professional woman, a reader, a thinker, a party girl, she was a woman I admired. When my father complained about our bonding on the basis that she was "funny," mama protested, insisting that "folks had a right to be who they are." When the gay man who lived across the street from us was cruelly teased and taunted by teenage boys, mama was there protesting, telling us that he was a responsible caring man — that we should respect and love him.

I was an advocate for gay rights long before I knew the word feminism. My family feared I was a lesbian long before they worried that I would never marry. And I was already on my way to being a true freak because I knew I would always choose to go where my blood beats, in any and all directions. When I wrote my first book, *Ain't I a Woman: Black Women and Feminism,* I had already been engaged in feminist movement which included straight, bisexual, and out gay women. We were young. And in those days there was pressure on some of us to prove we were really radically down with the movement by sharing our politics and our bodies with women. The lesson everybody learned in those days was that transgressive sexual practice did not make one politically progressive. When my first book came out and I was attacked by individual black lesbian women I was stunned. I was accused of being homophobic because there was no discussion of lesbianism in my book. That absence was not an indication of homophobia. I did not talk about sexuality in the book. I was not ready. I did not know enough. And had I known more I would have stated that so no one would have been able to label me homophobic.

What knowing powerful, caring lesbians taught me as a girl, a lesson that has continued, is that women do not need to depend on men for our well-being and our happiness — not even our sexual bliss. This knowledge opened up a world of possibility for women. It offered choice and options. We will never know how many millions of women stay in relationships with dominating sexist males simply because they cannot imagine a life where they can be happy without men, whether they are satisfied sexually and emotionally with the men in their life or not. If any female feels she needs anything beyond herself to legitimate and validate her existence, she is already giving away her power to be self-defining, her agency. Lesbian women inspired me from childhood on to claim the space of my own self-definition.

This is the special wisdom radical lesbian thinkers brought to feminist movement. Even if there were exceptional straight women who theoretically understood that one could be utterly fulfilled without the approval of men, without male erotic affirmation, they did not bring to the movement the lived experience of this belief. In the early stages of feminist movement we used the phrase "woman-identified woman" or "man-identified woman" to distinguish between those activists who did not choose lesbianism but who did choose to be woman-identified, meaning their ontological existence did not depend on male affirmation. Male-identified females were those who dropped feminist principles in a flash if they interfered with romantic heterosexual concerns. They were the females who also supported men more than women, who could always see things from the male perspective. Teaching one of my first women's studies courses in San Francisco I was confronted by a group of radical lesbian students who wanted to know why I was still "into" men. After class one day in the parking lot there was a showdown. At that time an older black woman lesbian student, who had worked in the sex industry, having much sexual intercourse with men even as she remained clear about her lesbian identity, defended my feminist honor by declaring, "she's a woman-identified woman who's into sex with men — that's her right, but she's still down with the cause."

Sustaining loyalty to feminist politics was a central topic of discussion within feminist circles by the mid-'80s as many women were dropping out. While visionary lesbian thinkers and/or activists had shaped the radical dimensions of the movement as women gained more rights, their presence, their input was often forgotten. Many of the lesbians who were most radical and courageous in the movement were from working-class backgrounds. Then they did not have the credentials needed to rise in academic circles. The academization of feminism reinscribed heterosexist hierarchies where straight women with fancy credentials were often given more respect and higher regard even if they had spent no time being involved in a women's movement outside the academy.

When it came to issues of difference, of expanding feminist theory and practice to include race and class, visionary lesbian thinkers were among those women most willing to change their perspectives. In many cases it was because they had an experiential understanding of what it means to be exploited and/or oppressed because you do not conform to mainstream standards. Visionary lesbians were far more willing to take on the issue of interrogating white supremacy than their straight comrades. And they were more likely to desire to strengthen bonds with all men. The vast majority of straight women, whether they were actively feminist or not, were more concerned about their relationships with men.

Our freedom as women to choose who we love, who we will share our bodies and lives with, has been deeply enhanced by the struggles of radical lesbian women both on behalf of gay rights and women's rights. Within feminist movement, both past and present-day, lesbians have always had to challenge and confront homophobia, much in the same way as all women of color irrespective of their sexual preference or identity challenged and confronted racism. Women who claim to be feminist while perpetuating homophobia are as misguided and hypocritical as those who want sisterhood while holding on to white supremacist thought.

Mainstream mass media has always chosen a straight woman to represent what the feminist movement stands for — the straighter the better. The more glamorous she is, the more her image can be used to appeal to men. Woman-identified women, whether straight, bisexual, or lesbian rarely make garnering male approval a priority in our lives. This is why we threaten the patriarchy. Lesbian women who have a patriarchal mindset are far less threatening to men than feminist women, gay or straight, who have turned their gaze and their desire away from the patriarchy, away from sexist men.

Nowadays the vast majority of lesbians, like their straight counterparts, are not into radical politics. Individual lesbian thinkers active in feminist movement often found it difficult to face the reality that lesbian women could be as sexist as straight women. The utopian notion that feminism would be the theory and lesbianism the practice was continually disrupted by the reality that most lesbians living in white supremacist capitalist patriarchal culture constructed partnerships using the same paradigms of domination and submission as did their heterosexual counterparts. And that building mutually satisfying bonds where no one risked being subordinated was as difficult to achieve in lesbian relationships as in heterosexual ones. The revelation that domestic violence happened in lesbian partnerships was the first clue that equality among women was not inherent in same sex bonds. Concurrently, feminist lesbians were far more willing to talk openly about their participation in sadomasochist sexual acts than their straight counterparts.

Sexually conservative feminists, gay and straight, found and continue to find consensual sexual rituals of domination and submission inappropriate and see them as betraying feminist ideals of freedom. Their absolute judgment, their refusal to respect the rights of all women to choose the sexual practice they find most fulfilling, is in actuality the stance which most undermines feminist movement. There are many women who will never understand what two women do together sexually, who will never desire another woman sexually, but who will always support the right of women to choose, to be lesbian or bisexual. That same support can be given lesbians and straight women who engage in sexual acts that would never appeal to most women or most people. Embedded in conservative feminist critique of lesbian sadomasochism was an underlying homophobia. Whenever any woman acts as though lesbians must always follow rigid moral standards to be deemed acceptable or to make straight people feel comfortable, they are perpetuating homophobia. Certainly as more straight women openly discussed their involvement with sexual sadomasochism, feminist critique was not as harsh and unrelenting as it was when it was seen as mostly a lesbian thing.

Challenging homophobia will always be a dimension of feminist movement. For there can be no sustained sisterhood between women when there is ongoing disrespect and subordination of lesbian females by straight women. In visionary feminist movement the work of activists who are lesbians is fully acknowledged. Without radical lesbian input feminist theory and practice would never have dared to push against the boundaries of heterosexism to create spaces where women, all women, irrespective of their sexual identity and/or preference, could and can be as free as they want to be. This legacy should be continually acknowledged and cherished.

17

TO LOVE AGAIN
The Heart of Feminism

If women and men want to know love, we have to yearn for feminism. For without feminist thinking and practice we lack the foundation to create loving bonds. Early on, profound disappointment with heterosexual relationships led many individual females to women's liberation. Many of these women felt betrayed by the promise of love and living happily ever after when they entered marriages with men who swiftly transformed themselves from charming princes into patriarchal lords of the manor. These heterosexual women brought to the movement their bitterness and their rage. They joined their heartache with that of lesbian women who had also felt betrayed in romantic bonds based on patriarchal values. As a consequence when it came to the issue of love the feminist take on the matter at the start of the movement was that female freedom could only happen if women let go their attachment to romantic love.

Our yearning for love, we were told in our consciousness-raising groups, was the seductive trap that kept us falling in love with patriarchal lovers, male or female, who used that love to subdue and subordinate us. Joining feminist movement before I had even had my first sexual experience with a man, I was stunned by the intense hatred and anger towards men that women expressed. Yet I understood the basis of the anger. My own conversion to feminist thinking in my teenage years was in direct response to my father's domination of everyone in our household. A military man, an athlete, a deacon of the church, a provider, a womanizer, he was the embodiment of patriarchal rule. I witnessed my mother's pain, and I rebelled. Mama never expressed anger or rage at gender injustice, no matter how extreme dad's humiliation of her or his violence.

When I went to my first consciousness-raising groups and heard women my mother's age give voice to pain, grief, and rage, their insistence that women had to move away from love made sense to me. But I still wanted the love of a good man, and I still believed I could find that love. However, I was absolutely certain that first the man had to be committed to feminist politics. In the early '70s, women who wanted to be with men faced the challenge of converting men to feminist thinking. If they were not feminist we knew there would be no lasting happiness.

Romantic love as most people understand it in patriarchal culture makes one unaware, renders one powerless and out of control. Feminist thinkers called attention to the way this notion of love served the interests of patriarchal men and women. It supported the notion that one could do anything in the name of love: beat people, restrict their movements, even kill them and call it a "crime of passion," plead, "I loved her so much I had to kill her." Love in patriarchal culture was linked to notions of possession, to paradigms of domination and submission wherein it was assumed one person would give love and another person receive it. Within patriarchy heterosexist bonds were formed on the basis that women being the gender in touch with caring emotions would give men love, and in return men, being in touch with power and aggression, would provide and protect. Yet in so many cases in heterosexual families men did not respond to care: instead they were tyrants who used their power unjustly to coerce and control. From the start heterosexual women came to women's liberation to stop the heartache — to break the bonds of love.

Significantly, they also stressed back then the importance of not living for one's children. This too was presented as another trap love set to prevent women from achieving full self-actualization. The mother, feminism warned us back then, who tried to vicariously live through her children, was a dominating, invasive monster capable of meting out cruel and unjust punishment. Those who came to feminist politics young were often rebelling against domineering mothers. We did not want to become them. We wanted our lives to be as different from their lives as we could make them. One way to ensure that we would be different would be simply to remain childless.

Early on the feminist critique of love was not complex enough. Rather than specifically challenging patriarchal misguided assumptions of love, it just presented love as the problem. We were to do away with love and put in its place a concern with gaining rights and power. Then, no one talked about the reality that women would risk hardening our hearts and end up being just as emotionally closed as the patriarchal men or butch females we were rejecting in the name of feminist rebellion. And for the most part this is exactly what happened. Rather than rethinking love and insisting on its importance and value, feminist discourse on love simply stopped. Women who wanted love, especially love with men, had to took elsewhere for an understanding of how they might find love. Many of those women turned away from feminist politics because they felt it denied the importance of love, of familial relations, of life lived in community with others.

Visionary feminist thinkers were also uncertain about what to say to women about love. In *Feminist Theory: From Margin to Center* I wrote about the need for feminist leaders to bring a spirit of love to feminist activism: "They should have the ability to show love and compassion, show this love through their actions, and be able to engage in successful dialogue." While I shared my belief that "love acts to transform domination" at that time I did not write in depth about the importance of creating feminist theory that would offer everyone a liberatory vision of love.

In retrospect it is evident that by not creating a positive feminist discourse on love, especially in relation to heterosexuality, we allowed patriarchal mass media to represent the entire movement as a politic grounded in hatred rather than love. Many females who wanted to bond with men felt that they could not nurture these ties and be committed to feminist movement. In actuality, we should have been spreading the word that feminism would make it possible for women and men to know love. We know that now.

Visionary feminism is a wise and loving politic. The soul of our politics is the commitment to ending domination. Love can never take root in a relationship based on domination and coercion. The radical feminist critique of patriarchal notions of love was not misguided. However, females and males needed more than a critique of where we had gone wrong on our journeys to love; we needed an alternative feminist vision. While many of us were coming to love in our private lives, a love rooted in feminist practice, we were not creating a broad-based feminist dialogue on love, one that would counter a focus on those factions within feminism that had been anti-love.

The heartbeat of our alternative vision is still a fundamental and necessary truth: there can be no love when there is domination. Feminist thinking and practice emphasize the value of mutual growth and self-actualization in partnerships and in parenting. This vision of relationships where everyone's needs are respected, where everyone has rights, where no one need fear subordination or abuse, runs counter to everything patriarchy upholds about the structure of relationships. Most of us have experienced or will experience male domination in our intimate private lives in relation to male parental caregivers, fathers, brothers, or, for heterosexual females, in romantic partnership. In actuality, the emotional well-being of women and men would be enhanced if both parties embrace feminist thinking and practice. A genuine feminist politics always brings us from bondage to freedom, from lovelessness to loving. Mutual partnership is the foundation of love. And feminist practice is the only movement for social justice in our society which creates the conditions where mutuality can be nurtured.

When we accept that true love is rooted in recognition and acceptance, that love combines acknowledgment, care, responsibility, commitment, and knowledge, we understand there can be no love without justice. With that awareness comes the understanding that love has the power to transform us, giving us the strength to oppose domination. To choose feminist politics, then, is a choice to love.

18

FEMINIST SPIRITUALITY

Feminism has been and continues to be a resistance movement which valorizes spiritual practice. Before I had feminist theory and practice to pull me fully into the awareness of the necessity of self-love and self-acceptance as necessary for self-actualization I walked on a spiritual path which affirmed those same messages. Despite the sexism of male-dominated religions females have found in spiritual practice a place of solace and sanctuary. Throughout the history of the church in Western life women have turned to monastic traditions to find a place for themselves where they can be with god without the intervention of men, where they can serve the divine without male domination. With keen spiritual insight and divine clarity the mystic Julian of Norwich would write long before the advent of contemporary feminism: "Our savior is our true Mother in whom we are endlessly born and out of whom we shall never come." Daring to counter the notion of our savior as always and only male Julian of Norwich was charting the journey back to the sacred feminine, helping to free women from the bondage of patriarchal religion.

Early on feminist movement launched a critique of patriarchal religion that has had a profound impact, changing the nature of religious worship throughout our nation. Exposing the way Western metaphysical dualism (the assumption that the world can always be understood by binary categories, that there is an inferior and a superior, a good and a bad) was the ideological foundation of all forms of group oppression, sexism, racism, etc., and that such thinking formed the basis of Judeo-Christian belief systems. To change how we worship then it was necessary to re-envision spirituality. Feminist critiques of patriarchal religion coincided with an overall cultural shift towards new age spirituality. Within new age spiritual circles practitioners were turning away from the fundamentalist Christian thought that had for centuries dominated Western psyches and looking towards the East for answers, for different spiritual traditions. Creation spirituality replaced a patriarchal spirituality rooted in notions of fall and redemption. In Hinduism, Buddhism, Voudoun, and diverse spiritual traditions women found images of female deities that allowed for a return to a vision of a goddess-centered spirituality.

Early on in feminist movement conflicts arose in response to those individual activists who felt the movement should stick to politics and take no stand on religion. A large number of the women who had come to radical feminism from traditional socialist politics were atheist. They saw efforts to return to a vision of sacred femininity as apolitical and sentimental. This divide within the movement did not last long as more women began to see the link between challenging patriarchal religion and liberatory spirituality. A huge majority of citizens in the United States identify themselves as Christian. More than other religious faith Christian doctrine which condones sexism and male domination informs all the ways we learn about gender roles in this society. Truly, there can be no feminist transformation of our culture without a transformation in our religious beliefs.

Creation-centered Christian spiritual awakening linked itself with feminist movement. In *Original Blessing* Matthew Fox explains:

"Patriarchal religions and patriarchal paradigms for religions have ruled the world's civilizations for at least 3,500 years. The creation-centered tradition is feminist. Wisdom and Eros counter more than knowledge or control in such spirituality." Speaking to the issue of tensions between feminists who are concerned with nature/ecology and those concerned with working for civil rights, shows that this is an unnecessary dualism:

> Political movements for justice are part of the fuller development of the cosmos, and nature is the matrix in which humans come to their self-awareness and their awareness of their power to transform. Liberation movements are a fuller development of the cosmos's sense of harmony, balance, justice, and celebration. This is why true spiritual liberation demands rituals of cosmic celebrating and healing, which will in turn culminate in personal transformation and liberation.

Liberation theologies see the liberation of exploited and oppressed groups as essential acts of faith reflecting devotion to divine will. Struggles to end patriarchy are divinely ordained.

Fundamentalist patriarchal religion has been and remains a barrier preventing the spread of feminist thought and practice. Indeed, no group has demonized feminists more than right-wing religious fundamentalists who have called for and condoned the murder of feminist thinkers, especially those who support women having reproductive rights. Initially, feminist critiques of Christianity separated masses of women from the movement. When feminist Christians began to offer new and creation-centered critiques and interpretations of the Bible, of Christian beliefs, however, women were able to reconcile their feminist politics and sustained commitment to Christian practice. However these activists have yet to fully organize a movement that addresses masses of Christian believers, converting them to an understanding that no conflict need exist be-

tween feminism and Christian spirituality. The same is true for those
feminists who are Jewish, Buddhist, Muslim, etc. Until that happens
organized patriarchal religion will always undermine feminist gains.

Initially contemporary feminism placed emphasis on civil
rights and material gains without giving enough attention to spiritu-
alism. Mainstream mass media called attention to feminist critiques
of religion but showed no interest in highlighting the spiritual awakening that occurred among diverse groups of feminist women.
Masses of people still think that feminism is anti-religion. In actuality feminism has helped transform patriarchal religious thought so
that more women can find a connection to the sacred and commit to
spiritual life.

Often feminist spiritual practice found acknowledgment and
acceptance in therapeutic settings where women were seeking to
heal from wounds inflicted by patriarchal assaults, many of which
took place within the family of origin or in relationships. And it was
in the context of feminist therapy that many women received affirmation for their spiritual quest. The private nature of this soul
searching often means that the public is not informed about the degree to which feminist activists now acknowledge fully the necessity
of attending to needs of the spirit — of spiritual life. In future feminist movement we will need better strategies for sharing information about feminist spirituality.

Choosing alternative spiritual paths has helped many women
sustain commitment to spiritual life even as they continue to challenge and interrogate patriarchal religion. The institutionalized patriarchal church or temple has been changed by feminist interventions.
But in more recent years the church has begun to abandon strides
made in the direction of gender equity. The rise in religious fundamentalism threatens progressive spirituality. Fundamentalism not
only encourages folks to believe that inequality is "natural," it per-

petuates the notion that control of the female body is necessary. Hence its assault on reproductive rights. Concurrently religious fundamentalism imposes on females and males repressive notions of sexuality which validate sexual coercion in many different forms. Clearly, there is still a need for feminist activists to highlight organized religion, to engage in ongoing critique and resistance.

While a world of wonderful, feminist-affirming spiritual traditions abound now, masses of people have no access to knowledge about these practices. They often feel that patriarchal religion is the only place where anyone cares about their spiritual well-being. Patriarchal religion has successfully used mass media, particularly television, to spread its message. Alternative spiritual paths must do likewise if we are to counter the notion that patriarchal religion is the only path. Feminist spirituality created a space for everyone to interrogate outmoded belief systems and created new paths. Representing god in diverse ways, restoring our respect for the sacred feminine, it has helped us find ways to affirm and/or re-affirm the importance of spiritual life. Identifying liberation from any form of domination and oppression as essentially a spiritual quest returns us to a spirituality which unites spiritual practice with our struggles for justice and liberation. A feminist vision of spiritual fulfillment is naturally the foundation of authentic spiritual life.

19

VISIONARY FEMINISM

To be truly visionary we have to root our imagination in our concrete reality while simultaneously imagining possibilities beyond that reality. A primary strength of contemporary feminism has been the way it has changed shape and direction. Movements for social justice that hold on to outmoded ways of thinking and acting tend to fail. The roots of visionary feminism extend back to the early '60s. At the very start of the women's liberation movement visionary thinkers were present dreaming about a radical/revolutionary political movement that would in its reformist stage grant women civil rights within the existing white supremacist capitalist patriarchal system while simultaneously working to undermine and overthrow that system. The dream was of replacing that culture of domination with a world of participatory economics grounded in communalism and social democracy, a world without discrimination based on race or gender, a world where recognition of mutuality and interdependency would be the dominant ethos, a global ecological vision of how the planet can survive and how everyone on it can have access to peace and well-being.

Radical/revolutionary feminist visions became clearer and more complex as the movement progressed. However they were often obscured by the absolutism of reformist feminists who really felt safer working for change solely within the existing social order. While some reformist feminist activists were really eager to change economic discrimination based on gender so that they could have equality with men of privileged classes, others just believed the movement would create more concrete relevant change in women's lives if energy was focused in the direction of reform. However ultimately forsaking the radical heartbeat of feminist struggle simply made the movement more vulnerable to cooptation by mainstream capitalist patriarchy.

Seduced by class power and/or greater class mobility once they made strides in the existing social order fewer women were interested in working to dismantle that system. On one hand while we are told again and again by individual feminist thinkers like Carol Gilligan and others that women are more caring, more ethical, the facts of how women conduct themselves in relation to less powerful women suggest otherwise. The ethics of care women show in the ethnic or racial groups with which they identify do not extend to those with whom they do not feel empathy, identification, or solidarity. Women of privilege (most of whom are white but not all) have rapidly invested in the sustained subordination of working-class and poor women.

A fundamental goal of visionary feminism was to create strategies to change the lot of all women and enhance their personal power. To do that, though, the movement needed to move way beyond equal rights agendas and start with basic issues like literacy campaigns that would embrace all women, but especially women of poorer groups. There is no feminist school, no feminist college. And there has been no sustained effort to create these institutions. Educated white women as the central beneficiaries of job and career-based affirmative action programs reaped benefits in the existing structures and were often not motivated to do the work of creating institutions based on feminist principles. These institutions could never pay high salaries. But even independently wealthy feminist activists have not used their money to fund educational programs that begin to work with women and girls who are disadvantaged when it comes to basic skills.

While visionary feminist thinkers have understood our need for a broad-based feminist movement, one that addresses the needs of girls and boys, women and men, across class, we have not produced a body of visionary feminist theory written in an accessible language or shared through oral communication. Today in academic circles much of the most celebrated feminist theory is written in a sophisticated jargon that only the well-educated can read. Most people in our society do not have a basic understanding of feminism; they cannot acquire that understanding from a wealth of diverse material, grade school–level primers, and so on, because this material does not exist. We must create it if we are to rebuild feminist movement that is truly for everyone.

Feminist advocates have not organized resources to ensure that we have television stations or consistent spots on any existing stations. There is no feminist news hour on any television or radio show. One of the difficulties we faced spreading the word about feminism is that anything having to do with the female gender is seen as covering feminist ground even if it does not contain a feminist perspective. We do have radio shows and a few television shows that highlight gender issues, but that it is not the same as highlighting feminism. Ironically one of the achievements of contemporary feminism is that everyone is more open to discussing gender and the concerns of women, but again, not necessarily from a feminist perspective. For example, feminist movement created the cultural revolution that made it possible for our society to face the problem of male violence against women and children.

Even though representations of domestic violence abound in mass media and discussions take place on every front, rarely does the public link ending male violence to ending male domination, to eradicating patriarchy. Most citizens of this nation still do not understand the link between male domination and male violence in the home. And that failure to understand is underscored as our nation is called upon to respond to violent murders of family members, friends, and schoolmates by young males of all classes. In mass media everyone raises the question of why this violence is taking place without linking it to patriarchal thinking.

Mass-based feminist education for critical consciousness is needed. Unfortunately class elitism has shaped the direction of feminist thought. Most feminist thinkers/theorists do their work in the elite setting of the university. For the most part we do not write children's books, teach in grade schools, or sustain a powerful lobby which has a constructive impact on what is taught in the public school. I began to write books for children precisely because I wanted to be a part of a feminist movement making feminist thought available to everyone. Books on tape help extend the message to individuals of all ages who do not read or write.

A collective door-to-door effort to spread the message of feminism is needed for the movement to begin anew, to start again with the basic premise that feminist politics is necessarily radical. And since that which is radical is often pushed underground in our setting then we must do everything we can to bring feminism above ground to spread the word. Because feminism is a movement to end sexism and sexist domination and oppression, a struggle that includes efforts to end gender discrimination and create equality, it is fundamentally a radical movement.

Confusion about this inherent radicalism emerged as feminist activists moved away from challenging sexism in all its manifestations and focused solely on reforms. Advancing the notion that there can be many "feminisms" has served the conservative and liberal political interests of women seeking status and privileged class power who were among the first group to use the term "power feminists." They also were the group that began to suggest that one could be feminist and be anti-abortion. This is another misguided notion. Granting women the civil right to have control over our bodies is a basic feminist principle. Whether an individual female should have an abortion is purely a matter of choice. It is not anti-feminist for us to choose not to have abortions. But it is a feminist principle that women should have the right to choose.

Parasitic class relations and the greed for wealth and power have led women to betray the interests of poor and working-class women. Women who once espoused feminist thinking now support public policies that are anti-welfare. They see no contradiction in this stance. They simply give their "brand" of feminism its own name. The representation of feminism as a lifestyle or a commodity automatically obscures the importance of feminist politics. Today many women want civil rights without feminism. They want the system of patriarchy to remain intact in the private sphere even as they desire equality in the public sphere. But visionary feminist thinkers have understood from the movement's inception that collusion with patriarchy, even patriarchal support of some aspects of feminist movement (i.e. the demand for women to work), will leave females vulnerable. We saw that rights gained without fundamental change in the systems that govern our lives could be easily taken away. And we are already seeing that happen in the arena of reproductive rights, particularly abortion. Giving civil rights within patriarchy has proved dangerous because it has led women to think that we are better off than we are, that the structures of domination are changing. In actuality those structures are re-entrenched as many women move away from feminism.

Extreme anti-feminist backlash has also undermined feminist movement. A significant part of the backlash is the bashing and trashing of feminism done by opportunistic, conservative women. For example: a recent book, *What Our Mothers Did Not Tell Us: Why Happiness Eludes the Modern Woman* by Danielle Crittendon, tells women that we should all stay home and mother to produce healthy children, that we should acknowledge basic differences in male and female psyches and that above all it is feminism that is at fault. Critics of feminism blame the movement for all the dissatisfaction modern women face. They never talk about patriarchy, male domination, racism, or class exploitation. While the anti-feminist books tend to be written in an accessible language that appeals to a broad readership, there is no body of popular feminist theory that serves as a counter to their message.

When I talk with radical feminists, especially those of us who are now in mid-life, between the ages of 35 and 65, I hear wonderful testimony about the constructive impact of feminism. It is essential that we document this work so that it stands as testimony countering the popular assumption that all feminism did was make the lives of women harder. Indeed it has made life far more complicated for women to have feminist thought and practice yet still remain within a patriarchal system of thought and action that is basically unchanged.

Visionary feminists have always understood the necessity of converting men. We know all the women in the world could become feminists but if men remain sexist our lives would still be diminished. Gender warfare would still be a norm. Those feminist activists who refuse to accept men as comrades in struggle — who harbor irrational fears that if men benefit in any way from feminist politics women lose — have misguidedly helped the public view feminism with suspicion and disdain. And at times man-hating females would rather see feminism not progress than confront the issues they have with men. It is urgent that men take up the banner of feminism and challenge patriarchy. The safety and continuation of life on the planet requires feminist conversion of men.

Feminist movement is advanced whenever any male or female of any age works on behalf of ending sexism. That work does not necessarily require us to join organizations; we can work on behalf of feminism right where we are. We can begin to do the work on feminism at home, right where we live, educating ourselves and our loved ones. In the past feminist movement has not provided individual females and male enough blueprints for change. While feminist politics are grounded in a firm set of beliefs about our purpose and direction, our strategies for feminist change must be varied.

There is no one path to feminism. Individuals from diverse backgrounds need feminist theory that speaks directly to their lives. As a black woman feminist thinker I find it essential to critically examine gender roles in black life to discover the specific concerns and strategies that must be addressed so that all black people can understand the relevance of feminist struggle in our lives.

Radical visionary feminism encourages all of us to courageously examine our lives from the standpoint of gender, race, and class so that we can accurately understand our position within the imperialist white supremacist capitalist patriarchy. For years many feminist women held to the misguided assumption that gender was the sole factor determining their status. Breaking through this denial was a crucial turning point for feminist politics. It enabled women to face the way biases of race and class had led to the formation of a women's movement that was not mass-based.

We are now ready to renew feminist struggle. Anti-feminist backlash exists because the movement was successful at showing everyone the threat patriarchy poses to the well-being of females and males. If feminist movement had not offered a true accounting of the dangers of perpetuating sexism and male domination, it would have failed. There would have been no need to mount an anti-feminist campaign. While patriarchal mass media continues to spread the lie that males are not welcome in the feminist classroom, truthfully more males are studying feminist thought and converting to feminist thinking. It is this significant change in feminist movement that makes it more of a threat to patriarchy. As has been stated, had the movement only focused on women, the patriarchal status quo would be intact and there would be no need to severely bash feminism.

We are told again and again by patriarchal mass media, by sexist leaders, that feminism is dead, that it no longer has meaning. In actuality, females and males of all ages, everywhere, continue to grapple with the issue of gender equality, continue to seek roles for themselves that will liberate rather than restrict and confine; and they continue to turn towards feminism for answers. Visionary feminism offers us hope for the future. By emphasizing an ethics of mutuality and interdependency feminist thinking offers us a way to end domination while simultaneously changing the impact of inequality. In a universe where mutuality is the norm, there may be times when all is not equal, but the consequence of that inequality will not be subordination, colonization, and dehumanization.

Feminism as a movement to end sexism, sexist exploitation, and oppression is alive and well. While we do not have a mass-based movement, the renewal of such a movement is our primary goal. To ensure the continued relevance of feminist movement in our lives visionary feminist theory must be constantly made and re-made so that it addresses us where we live, in our present. Women and men have made great strides in the direction of gender equality. And those strides towards freedom must give us strength to go further. We must courageously learn from the past and work for a future where feminist principles will undergird every aspect of our public and private lives. Feminist politics aims to end domination to free us to be who we are — to live lives where we love justice, where we can live in peace. Feminism is for everybody.

INDEX

About South End Press

South End Press is a nonprofit, collectively run book publisher with more than 200 titles in print. Since our founding in 1977, we have tried to meet the needs of readers who are exploring, or are already committed to, the politics of radical social change. Our goal is to publish books that encourage critical thinking and constructive action on the key political, cultural, social, economic, and ecological issues shaping life in the United States and in the world. In this way, we hope to give expression to a wide diversity of democratic social movements and to provide an alternative to the products of corporate publishing.

Through the Institute for Social and Cultural Change, South End Press works with other political media projects — Z magazine; Speakout, a speakers' bureau; and Alternative Radio — to expand access to information and critical analysis.

Other South End Press Titles
by bell hooks

Ain't I a Woman: Black Women and Feminism	$15
Black Looks: Race and Representation	$15
Breaking Bread: Insurgent Black Intellectual Life (with Cornel West)	$16
Feminist Theory: From Margin to Center (Second Edition)	$16
Sisters of the Yam: Black Women and Self-Recovery	$15
Talking Back: Thinking Feminist, Thinking Black	$15
Yearning: Race, Gender, and Cultural Politics	$17

To order, please send a check or money order to: South End Press, 7 Brookline Street, #1, Cambridge, MA 02139-4146. To order by credit card, call 1-800-533-8478. Please include $3.50 for postage and handling for the first book and 50 cents for each additional book. Write to receive a free catalog (southend@southendpress.org), or visit our web site, http://www.southendpress.org